PRAISE FOR *WORK TRIBES*

"*Work Tribes* gets to the heart of great leadership: helping your teams do great work together by creating caring, collaborative, and fulfilling work environments. Shawn's latest is an exceptional handbook for anyone looking to improve their leadership and the lives of those in their span of care!" —BOB CHAPMAN,
CEO, Barry-Wehmiller;
author of *Everybody Matters*

"We've measured and talked about employee engagement for decades, and the numbers haven't moved. Shawn Murphy has discovered the missing piece: establishing a sense of belonging. *Work Tribes* turned my thinking on its ear many times—in a powerful way!" —KAREN MARTIN,
President, TKMG; author of *Clarity First*
and *The Outstanding Organization*

"The pursuit of joy in the context of work is a noble yet, for many, elusive pursuit. Perhaps it is because we are ignoring the importance of the invisible, yet critical, elements of true teamwork: chemistry and relationships. In my own pursuit of creating a high-performing work culture, I have always been intrigued by the idea of tribes and the image it conjures of a tight-knit community, working shoulder to shoulder, family lives, and work lives intertwined, sustained by campfire stories and strong traditions. In *Work Tribes*, Shawn Murphy pulls the curtain back on the invisible and shows us what it takes to build strong, high-performing, cohesive teams that last. You want this where you work. You know you do. First step: read this book. Then get going!"
—RICH SHERIDAN,
CEO, Menlo Innovations;
author of *Joy, Inc.* and *Chief Joy Officer*

WORK TRIBES

The SURPRISING SECRET to BREAKTHROUGH PERFORMANCE, ASTONISHING RESULTS, and KEEPING TEAMS TOGETHER

SHAWN MURPHY

HarperCollins
Leadership

AN IMPRINT OF HARPERCOLLINS

Work Tribes

Published by HarperCollins Leadership, an imprint of HarperCollins Focus LLC.

Any internet addresses, phone numbers, or company or product information printed in this book are offered as a resource and are not intended in any way to be or to imply an endorsement by HarperCollins Leadership, nor does HarperCollins Leadership vouch for the existence, content, or services of these sites, phone numbers, companies, or products beyond the life of this book.

ISBN 978-0-8144-3996-8 (eBook)
ISBN 978-0-8144-3995-1 (HC)

Library of Congress Cataloging-in-Publication Data

Library of Congress Control Number: 2019934400

Printed in the United States of America

19 20 21 22 23 LSC 5 4 3 2 1

To Dad

When the universe said reach out, I did.

And you were there.

Rest in Peace, 2019

CONTENTS

INTRODUCTION

For over 200,000 years the human species has survived harsh environments. Our adaptability and persistence in finding ways to live a good life has allowed us to evolve from surviving to thriving. The lessons our hairy ancestors used to create societies and communities are still encoded in our brains. For example, we have always been social creatures. The comfort of friendships and the safety from being part of a community were and still are powerful forces shaping our human experience.

It is a bit peculiar that in our long history as a human race we have not fully embraced how our human needs can transform the way we work and how we lead people. It is as if their instructive nature and indelible influence on our actions and interactions were simply ignored.

Our human needs have shaped societies throughout the course of time. Our curiosity and desires have helped build empires. The same impulses and behaviors have collapsed them, as well. Yet, we have not fully teased out the better parts of our needs and intentionally directed them to create truly human workplaces, a workplace that satisfies more than a need for money, power, or recognition.

In fact, there is a surprising secret that is biologically imbedded in each of us. This surprise is not one that needs training to understand. Nor does it require an advanced degree to explain. Our human needs have one particular secret that shapes how we view ourselves and our place in this world, personally and professionally.

What is this surprising secret?

It is belonging.

At work, the need to feel like we belong is a dynamic and powerful influence on people, performance, and results. It dramatically improves the employee experience, your company and team cultures, and even deeply enriches the work you do.

To study belonging at work, my research partner, Bruce Elliot, and I met with employees in companies featured throughout this book. We wanted to understand how belonging at work is created and sustained in teams or companies. Throughout the book you will learn from companies and individuals what they do to shape belonging.

When Bruce and I were analyzing the interview data, we struggled to answer a nagging question: How does belonging scale in an organization? In other words, how can a company create a sense of belonging across the company, no matter the size of the business, the location of its workforce, or even the tools used to help people work?

Despite the positive attributes belonging at work has, Bruce and I struggled to answer the scaling question. But then it dawned on us. Belonging is not a corporate strategy that you roll out. There is no corporate mandate from the CEO that inspires belonging. Instead, belonging is an outcome. It is shaped by the interactions and dynamics between people and groups of people.

The good news about shaping belonging is that you can do so with intention. And that is what this book is about. As a leader of people, you will learn ways to inspire a sense of belonging for your team. There is no need to be a psychologist to understand human nature. You merely need to be willing to improve the place we spend the majority of our day, at work. A dash of curiosity, compassion, and vulnerability will also help. In short, relate to colleagues as people and not a resource who gets work done.

There is a small trend emerging in companies like LinkedIn and Airbnb. They have senior leaders responsible for belonging at work. The responsibility often goes to the diversity and inclusion leader. It's a logical conclusion, and perhaps the right one. But be wary of turning belonging into what diversity and inclusion (D&I) practices have become. D&I has become a program. It can come with quotas—hire this many African American women. It becomes a number that is reported out to investors; Facebook and other tech companies publicly share how diverse their workforce is or is not. In a way D&I has become a program to help counter our bias to surround and hire people who are like us.

Belonging is not diversity. It has everything to do with university. The original Latin meaning of diversity focuses on separateness. That separateness is expressed by focusing on variety and differences. While there is nothing wrong with diversity, the original meaning of the word and how it is viewed, at least within the workplace, is predominately a focus on dissimilarities. We need diverse people and ways of thinking in and out of the workplace. Yet, to focus on our differences creates an imbalance in how we view one another. The separateness creates division, an unnecessary competition for superiority. We do, indeed, need diversity in teams. Not just in the typical areas—race, gender, sexual orientation—but also in how people think.

Cognitive diversity is also important—the intentional selection of people who approach problem solving in different ways. It's a way to temper our own bias of hiring people who think like we do.

Opposite of diversity is university. Let's turn again to Latin for the definition of university. The word university shifts its focus to, well, the universe, or the whole, the original definition.

Notice the nuance. Rather than focus on how we are different, belonging, an example of university, satisfies a deeper need than standing out. University emphasizes the reassuring feeling of place and identity.

Where diversity focuses on differences that separate us, university seeks to view humanity as one whole or the entirety of the human existence. For some this might seem a bit high-brow or lofty. After all, we're just talking about work, right? On a foundational level, yes. But, for most employees—hired or appointed—work is hardly foundational. It is a significant influence on their identity, their livelihood, the expression of their intellect. We cannot achieve on our own feats of brilliance. Only through a team, unit, or company can the impossible be tackled.

When I started my corporate career in 1990, the prevailing wisdom was friends at work are distractions. The assumed logic was when you are at work, no personal phone calls, keep conversations to a minimum, and your child care issues need to be handled before coming to work. This draconian mindset was and is still ill-fitting for the workplace. The mindset still exists today.

It is seductive to think belonging will ease what ails our organizations. Unfortunately, I cannot deliver to you false promises. In the simple and in the spectacular, hard work is always nearby. The model companies and their employees' stories featured here are fraught with tension, the tension between business needs and human drives and needs. I do not want to oversell the difficult work of creating a space and place where people feel safe, comfortable exploring their skills and applying their experience. I wrote this book to strongly nudge you to take on the responsibility of connecting with what makes us human to achieve astonishing results. So, know this: When you accept the premise that belonging holds teams together, you have overcome quite possibly the hardest hurdle—doubt. With an eye on keeping it real and balanced, when you read part 2 you will learn about the barriers and problems inherent with creating a sense of belonging at work. Though hard work is involved, it is made easier when you enlist your team to your vision of an experience of work that moves and inspires.

Belonging is beautiful. It is messy. To experience belonging means you will go through a range of emotions. When your team succeeds you celebrate together. When a team member acts selfishly you discuss it and move on. The relationships that create and emerge from belonging are hardly perfect.

When true belonging holds a team together the drama and messiness from working together are more deeply understood. Instead of maligning a person belonging guides teams to understand one another and be bolder in how they hold one another accountable.

In the end, I hope you find that belonging isn't an initiative you start at work. Rather, belonging becomes an outcome you intentionally nurture. I'm happy to show you how.

WORK TRIBES

PART I

AN UNFORGETTABLE EXPERIENCE

CHAPTER I

HIDDEN CURRENTS

The Irresistible Tug of Belonging and Why It Matters at Work

By thinking human nature is monolithic, we instantly limit our potential.

—Michael Puett and Christine Gross-Loh[1]

The scene is a diner in Omaha, Nebraska, in 1959. A typical busy night of families and travelers enjoying their meals is suddenly interrupted by a man falling out of his booth and lying on the diner floor in a fit of uncontained laughter. The man, Charlie, is responding to something his friend Warren had said from where he sits across the table with his wife. Charlie's own wife, who is sitting at his side, does not look nearly as amused while witnessing him rolling on the floor laughing.

That night at the diner really happened. It was early in what has become one of today's most-respected, successful business partnerships and lifelong friendships. The two men at the diner were Charlie Munger and Warren Buffett, partners at the esteemed Berkshire Hathaway. Sixty years later, Warren and Charlie are still friends and speak repeatedly every day. In short, these highly successful businessmen have an unwavering friendship.[2]

Munger and Buffett are notorious in business and leadership circles for their commonsense business principles. Yet, for two very wealthy men who are clearly talented with money and investing, they have maintained an enduring respect for Berkshire Hathaway managers and their respective teams. Regarding the leaders of the company, Buffett wrote in the company's 2010 letter to shareholders, "Our trust is in people rather than process. A 'hire well, manage little' code suits both them and me."[3]

It is tempting to expand by way of evidence a revelatory explanation of how the notorious business leaders' friendship contributes to success. I could discuss the fortunes Munger and Buffett have made and have helped others make as a result of a long history of great chemistry. Or retell stories from Buffett's biographer, Alice Schroeder, that demonstrate the humanity and humility underlying the billionaire's personality. Instead of examining the outcomes of such a great partnership, this book will focus on the lessons we can learn from what contributes to such abundance—materially and emotionally. As a leader, you are measured by your successes. However, the savviest among us know that orchestrating the convergence of talents in our people is the "secret sauce" to success.

The secret sauce has a name: human chemistry. One of the first people to use this term was Thomas Dreier in 1948. Dreier labeled leaders as human chemists. "Think of yourself first of all as a human chemist. Look upon your office as a laboratory . . . [Elements'] natures are such that alone they can serve only certain purposes; but when skillfully united with other elements their usefulness is broadened by the kind and number of elements with which they are mixed."[4] Dreier goes on to say that the outcome of a leader's know-how to tap into human chemistry is wholly dependent on the chemist.[5]

One element that I believe all great human chemists use is deeply embedded in our humanity—belonging. Using this potentially volatile element requires understanding how it emerges and what it takes to facilitate it in the first place. Of course, it is important to know what kind of cultures can "blow up" belonging too.

How ludicrous that some leaders hold on to the outdated belief that the workplace is no place to build meaningful friendships. The denial of collegial chemistry is unnatural. Our human nature has evolved over hundreds of thousands of years, and yet some elements of being human have not changed. For example, we are drawn to people who are like us. Both Munger and Buffett have acknowledged that what drew them together were similarities in how they viewed life, their high regard for their fathers, and a whip-smart business acumen. The head buzz that comes from clicking with others smooths interactions, making it easier to avoid feeling annoyed or getting hooked by idiosyncratic behaviors and differing beliefs. The hidden currents between people need not only be sexual.

As in Munger and Buffett's case, friendship is a deeply positive influence. "Too often, a vast collection of possessions ends up possessing its owner. The asset I most value, aside from health, is interesting, diverse, and long-standing friends," says Buffett.[6]

The hidden currents that tug at us, bringing us together or repelling us like two magnetic positive charges, are too often overlooked at work. We make complex meaning out of workplace culture, holding it up as the crown jewel of what makes a positive experience at work. But too many companies that want to be esteemed employers fail to grasp the significant influence deeply gratifying friendships have on people and performance. If you want a great culture, you need employees to build high-quality relationships with one another. Without meaningful work relationships your company's culture has no character, no magnetism.

Consider for a moment the amount of time and money invested in employee engagement or improving employee morale. In a 2012 study, companies spent $720 million on engagement solutions.[7] Yet in 2018, nearly 66 percent of US workers were still disengaged.[8] Reduced to shortcuts and popular "culture tricks," leaders invest in indoor slides, beer walls, breakfast bars, and free dry cleaning, believing these perks matter. These entertaining elements are fun until an underskilled manager fails to advocate for his team. The deterioration of relationships or the absence of quality ones will diminish the effectiveness of culture tricks. The simplest solutions are always the hardest to see. While companies distractedly look for quick hits to make employees "happy," "motivated," "satisfied," or whatever current business colloquialism dominates popular wisdom, the secret sauce is largely unused.

Can you move a mountain by pushing it with your bare hands? The rational side of your brain says, "of course not!" But consider for a moment that your logic is undermining your perceptions. Yes, mountains are monolithic. (If you look up the definition of *monolithic*, you'll find that it has some nuanced meanings associated with something that is so big it is imposing, rigid, and fails to be interesting.)[9] But if you hear my question without the filter of logic, you could find a way to move a mountain with your bare hands. You could, for example, use your hands to direct a massive earth-mover, which reduces the stature of the mountain. A logical response to my question hides possibilities from your view. Conversely, challenging your mind's immediate response reveals them. These possibilities show themselves through an openness to other perspectives. They also allow us to experience a broader spectrum of emotions and even observe the depths of our unique expressions of creativity.

The curious leaders who routinely seek ways to remain relevant and use effective methods to achieve mutually beneficial results will quickly learn how to create an unforgettable experience of work. What it takes for leaders to inspire and motivate today's workforce is wholly rooted in human nature. To fully grasp this paradigm shift requires that you challenge convenient beliefs.

A convenient belief is one that lets us off the hook. When we quickly, perhaps blindly, settle for what has always been we are relying on conventional thinking. Leadership and conventional business thinking is not enough to generate the value any company wants to deliver. In a time where technology advancements and their influence on the workforce worry many thinkers, leaders, and employees, we need to learn how to use the good in our human nature to design an unforgettable experience of work. We need not throw out the proverbial bath water with the baby. We need a better mix of longstanding business conventionalities that remain steadfast in their effectiveness, along with evolving our thinking about leadership and the role work plays in our lives.

Logic is hardly enough when it comes to making sense of our human nature. Looking at and making sense of work through what it means to be human can be confusing. After all, for centuries we built companies on the belief that work is a means to a monetary end, without much thought for the actual workers. Employers were the big "baddies." (Perhaps monolithic?) Companies paid a meager wage and expected outrageous results with limited time and resources. (Some things do not change.) There was no concern for employees' personal challenges or professional goals. Humanity was hardly a factor in designing how the business generated value. Instead, the prevailing viewpoint was this: "You get a paycheck for a month's worth of work. Suck it up buttercup; your paycheck is gratitude enough. You're lucky to have a job."

Human nature is hardly monolithic. It is diverse, outrageous, expansive, and simple—simultaneously. With advances in psychology, neuroscience, biology, and many other "ologies," we now have deeper insights into how our brain helps us make sense of the world, others around us, and ourselves. Science has also revealed insights that help us understand our own narrative as human beings. We will hear later from scientists and their research to learn how to become master mixers of human chemistry.

What does human nature have to do with business and leadership? Throughout our time on earth, we have always worked alongside others out of a need to survive and find enjoyment. Today we have built upon these instincts a nuanced knowledge of what facilitates great working partnerships. Our quest for ways to live a fulfilling life has merged into our professional pursuits. What it means to be human has always quietly shaped our work, the solutions we help create, and the relationships we nourish with those who also contribute to the work. We are now beginning to see the value of being human at work. Science and experience have led us to this point—human-centric workplaces are a natural evolution in the ways businesses generate value. More importantly, our human nature has deepened our need to evolve how we lead people, teams, groups, and ourselves. The organizations that ignore this will become irrelevant, undesirable, and forgettable.

THE TUG OF BELONGING

Just a few years after Buffett and Munger became good friends in Omaha, the same bonding agent was weaving its influence on two musicians, but this time in London. When Mick Jagger and Keith Richards shared a fateful train ride into London on October 17, 1960, a powerful chemistry worked its influence on the two young wannabe musicians. At the time neither future superstar realized that a lifelong friendship was beginning. The two future Rolling Stones band members had discovered that they shared a longing for a different type of music than was popular in the United Kingdom in the early sixties. For Jagger and Richards, they could not get enough of the blues coming from US artists like Chuck Berry, Buddy Holly, and Richie Valens. Their earnest passion and shared commitment to learn to play the blues and to find a way to express themselves helped form one of the greatest rock bands ever.[10]

What bonding agent brought these two sets of friends together in completely different working environments? The Rolling Stones was created out of a contagious chemistry between Jagger and Richards. Likewise, Berkshire Hathaway's prodigious success is partially rooted in the undeniable chemistry between Buffett and Munger. Human chemistry is what helps facilitate the awareness that working with others "just feels right." But what is human chemistry? What can be learned from it so its advantages can be useful in business?

Human chemistry is more than a feeling. It is biologically wired into our brains, and its influence can be experienced in our physical body. Neuroscience provides an explanation for why we jell with others through what scientists call limbic resonance. Think of limbic resonance as your body's environmental antenna. You are constantly surveying your environment, picking up cues so you can make sense of what is happening around you: Why is there tension in the meeting? Should you be worried? Is the tension linked to why one colleague has his arms crossed and the others are ignoring him? Your limbic brain takes in these signals through sight, sound, smells, and feelings and then tells the other parts of your brain to respond. Limbic resonance is a capacity that stems from the limbic region of your brain. Because of the constant surveying and meaning-making of your environment, you have developed the capacity to synchronize mentally with others. This is limbic resonance. It is a powerful capacity that shapes the strength and nature of your relationships. High-quality relationships have a positive limbic resonance and contribute to the chemistry between you and others.[11]

Perhaps not always perceptible or easy to point out, the need to belong is an undercurrent that electrifies the connections we make. It bonds with human chemistry in a compelling manner. It does not matter the context, the type of work, the industry, or even education levels, the tug of belonging can be intentionally inspired and cultivated.

Two fundamental habits separate humans from other forms of life—attachment and caregiving. Attachment to our parents leads to the first relationship we develop. Our young brains are shaped and structured by the patterns of words, tones of voices, and body language. It is through communication that we developed our need to connect with others. Dr. Dan Siegal, clinical professor of psychiatry at UCLA, points out that communication is what helped our ancestors, and now us, to move from an individual perspective to a "we" perspective.[12] Our communities evolved, and so did our brains, from our ability to share ideas, expand on them, and express our feelings with other human beings.

Caregiving, the second fundamental habit, became necessary to help families collectively raise children. Out of necessity we learned as a human race that cooperation helped build stronger relationships and communities. Cooperation is the glue between attachment and caregiving.

To help us understand the science behind belonging, let's look at Dr. Siegal's work, which has helped us understand the invisible currents between ourselves and others. From research conducted at the Foundation for Psychocultural Research/UCLA Center for Culture, Brain, and Development, Siegal and his colleagues have learned that life experiences shape our brain's neural structures. And the most formative experiences on our lives are social relationships. "They literally form who we are," says Siegal.[13] Relationships are also central to our well-being. Quality relationships in our lives help us live with purpose, find and make meaning, have compassion, and find our place in this world. As Siegal puts it, relationships are the most important influence on a life well-lived.[14]

The amplification of high-quality work relationships develops extraordinary value for customers and the business. You will read how companies like Airbnb, LinkedIn, The Container Store, and one of the most successful, popular restaurants in Seattle, Canlis Restaurant, lean on belonging to achieve stellar outcomes as places where employees want to be.

THE ARCHITECTURE
OF BELONGING

It's been over six decades since psychologist Abraham Maslow placed the need for belonging on his "hierarchy of needs" pyramid. Maslow believed that for any human to achieve self-actualization, he or she needed to satisfy the need to have relationships that were fulfilling and meaningful. Fast forward to the mid-90s, psychologists Roy F. Baumeister and Mark R.

Leary hypothesized that our human need to belong is a significant motivation that affects how we think and feel about ourselves and how we view others.[15]

In 2012, sociologist Dr. Brené Brown contributed to the scientific understanding of belongingness by distinguishing that it has nothing to do with fitting in. In her book *Defying Greatly*, Brown explains that fitting in is a barrier to belonging: "Fitting in is about assessing a situation and becoming who you need to be in order to be accepted."[16] Belonging is the antithesis of this. When we believe we belong, we quiet any doubts about our place in a team, family, among friends, and even in a community.

I define *belonging* as "feeling valued, wanted, and welcomed." Belonging is what tingles your senses and signals that you are okay, that you are safe. It helps you relax your defenses and genuinely engage with others. It assuages doubts and fears linked to acceptance. It has been said that diversity is being invited to a party and inclusion is being asked to dance. Well, belonging is what brought you to the party in the first place.

Across centuries of human history, belonging has been central to our survival. We have an enduring need to connect with, feel loyalty to, and believe in the security of our relationships—that we are accepted as individuals. Belonging facilitates getting work done and tending to the constant demands of living. We develop a social identity of who we are.[17]

Consider for a moment the way your relationships at work shape how you view yourself. Do they motivate you to do your best and, consequently, feel good about yourself? Perhaps you feel uncertainty about your relationship with your boss because he is rarely available? Or you wonder if you are really part of the team because in some way you are different from the others? The worry, doubt, or simply having no answer to the question, "Do I belong here?" is mentally distracting. This nagging question, subconsciously or consciously, occupies your cognitive abilities. It prevents you from doing your best work, sharing your ideas, and even developing authentic relationships with your teammates. To feel as though you belong or, worse, feel as though you do not, shapes your identity. And in the business world, you do not have time to wonder if who you are and what you bring to the team is valued and wanted. Momentum, progress, and results are central to a successful career and experience of work. Belonging is not just a "nice to have" characteristic of company culture. It is a source of vitality to high-performing people and organizations.

WORK THAT MATTERS

Today's workplace is not your parent's workplace. Yet an over-supply of managers unknowingly follows a leadership recipe that emphasizes compliance over commitment. An effective leadership recipe is guided by a set of actions that promote a growth mindset. Such a mindset is characterized by the belief that you and others can expand skill sets through continuous learning.[18] Foundational to a growth mindset is the belief that humans have unlimited potential. We merely need to learn how to inspire others to explore what they are capable of, even if it's associated with something new or different. As a leader of people, it is essential to help employees fulfill their potential. Anything short of this outcome is not enough to support people in bringing their preferred self to work or to influence a sense of belonging.

For decades researchers have compared what employees want from their work to what their leaders believe is important. Despite an abundance of research, books, workshops, conferences, blog posts, magazine articles, and even personal testimonies from fellow leaders, a chasm of confusion still exists. On one side of the chasm are leaders. Leaders continue to incorrectly place money and benefits as most important to employees. On the other side of the too-wide-gap are employees. To them a positive experience of work is most important: a supportive culture, meaningful work relationships, and growth opportunities.

As long as leaders and employees continue to stare across the chasm at one another, companies essentially limit their relevance and attractiveness to top talent. Top talent today wants to do work that matters *and* receive fair compensation. These two are table stakes for an attractive employment value proposition.

To avoid the disconnects from an outdated employment value proposition, I want to position you to understand the advantages of belonging at work. More important than that, however, is that I want to show you how to become a human chemist who knows which elements help belonging to emerge. To start, there are five advantages that help link the interpersonal benefits of belonging to business needs.

Advantage One:
Organization and Individual Performance Increases

A significant influence on belonging is caring. If you believe your boss and colleagues care about you, it will be easier to find your place in the team. Remove the distraction of your inner voice whispering, "It's not safe. Be careful," and you can more confidently apply your strengths and talents to your work. Correspondingly, trust becomes a bonding agent that eases team dynamics, promotes team cohesion, and facilitates getting things done.

In 2017, Ed Frauenheim from Great Place to Work (GPTW), the organization that produces the annual Top 100 Best Places to Work list, cowrote a *Fortune* blog post with me on the business benefits of caring and belonging. We revealed that the relationship between caring and trust significantly influences employee and organization performance. From GPTW's research findings, employees in caring, high-trust work environments are 44 percent more likely to work for a company with above-average revenue growth.[19] Overlay this insight with talent strategies, and a serious competitive advantage emerges that is hard to duplicate. Consider the reputation a company develops when it is known to have a caring work environment. The reputation helps attract highly desirable talent. We all want to know how we are performing. Leaders in such companies regularly focus on growing their employees' skills and continuously tapping into their strengths. Since caring and belonging are outcomes from diligent attention to creating a positive experience of work, there already exists a focus on performance. To care about employees and to create the conditions for them to believe they are valued, wanted, and welcomed is deeply rooted in performance.

Returning to GPTW's research, caring and belonging was found to hold more value to employees than a company's strategy, innovation, and managements' leadership competency. The research institute's findings about caring parallel the value of belonging. Consider that the revenue growth from a caring and collegial environment benefited from these drivers:

- People care about each other here.
- Management hires people who fit in well here.
- You can count on people to cooperate.
- There is a "family" or "team" feeling here.
- This is a fun place to work.[20]

The win-win outcomes listed above position the organization to achieve greater levels of success by tapping into the humanity of belonging and caring. In today's disruptive business environment, organizations must adapt to remain relevant and consistently deliver value to customers. Retaining high performers is one way to help companies make good on their value proposition. A way to retain employees is to show them that they are needed and valued.

Advantage Two:
Employee Motivation Is More Sustainable

Picture your boss at work. For the sake of this example, let us assume that you believe he or she is genuinely interested in you and your success. Additionally, you think that the company values your contributions and cares about your well-being. We do not need academic validation to know that we positively respond when we are treated fairly and kindly. This is a logical conclusion for most—treat me right and I will do the same to you. So how does this influence your motivation?

Researchers in social cognitive neuroscience have studied the regions of the brain believed to be affected by our social needs like belonging. What they discovered is when we are pleased with our relationships, the brain responds to the positive feedback in the same way it does to monetary rewards. The main difference between the two is that relationships have a long-lasting influence on our willingness to do our best. It turns out that our evolution as humans has wired our brains to place greater importance on relationships.[21] Relationships are core to human functioning. Although money is key to surviving, relationships are central to us thriving in life and at work. High-quality connections, a topic we'll explore in more detail later, motivate us to want to be our best self. Would you not feel grateful to have a respectful work relationship with your boss as referenced in the mini-scenario above? Going one step further, would you be more mindful of doing your best work out of respect for the high-quality relationship? When you believe your boss and your team have your back, the experience motivates you to want to maintain these positive social relations. As a leader, if you're going to find ways to motivate your team to perform at higher levels, you will need to create a positive work environment and place a high value on social reliance—employees relying on each other to get things done.

Advantage Three:
Employee Well-Being Improves

When Susan (not her real name) pushed the cake in Janet's face (not her real name), the party in the office breakroom quickly ended. Their manager had to intervene between the two women to ensure the situation did not escalate. The cake fight was the outcome of months of microaggressions between Susan and Janet. Their behavior towards one another had devolved into snarky remarks said under their breath, gossiping about each other to colleagues, and Susan even hiding Janet's notebook and making her think she misplaced it. The collapse of respect for one another and their peers led to sleepless nights, increased stress, strained personal relationships, and a rollercoaster of emotional highs and lows.

Strained work relationships have been linked to less physically and psychologically healthy people. Research finds that people who are socially isolated have a higher mortality rate compared to those with high-quality relationships. And the findings get worse. People who do not have quality social connections are more likely to be obese, smoke, and have high blood pressure.[22]

There is good news, however. When we have meaningful social connections, we flourish. Our life expectancy increases. Our immune systems get a positive boost. Psychological health and self-esteem improve. We are more empathetic, more trusting, and more willing to collaborate with others. Imagine how your employees could benefit from a sense of belonging contributed, in part, by enjoying working alongside their colleagues.[23] You can influence this positive outcome by fostering a sense of belonging.

Advantage Four:
The Experience of Work Is More Fulfilling

For the majority of people, work falls dramatically short of being a fulfilling experience. Work is a place nearly 70 percent of people do not want to be.[24] It would be logical to conclude that nobody wants to be at work, because, well, it is work. That conclusion is oversimplified. If we turn to human needs for insights, a more comprehensive and disturbing picture emerges.

First, the primary need for safety sheds light on why work is not fulfilling. Consider the trend of rising incivility at work, explained by Christine Porath, associate professor of management at Georgetown University. Porath reveals that over the past two decades, there has been a 50 percent increase in incivility at work.[25]

A quick Google search reveals a definition of incivility as rude or unsociable speech or behavior. In Porath's research, 98 percent of workers polled say they experience incivility at least weekly. Employees cannot feel safe when they are disrespected or worse. The distraction of uncivil behavior diminishes any chance of fulfillment from work. A key contributor to incivility is a lack of compassion for others, resulting in toxic relationships. A sense of belonging is not possible when incivility and toxicity go unchecked. If the degraded quality of work relationships is not persuasive enough to make safety a priority at work, Porath's research uncovers a list of nasty outcomes that undermine organization performance. Of those who experienced uncivil behavior at work:

- 48 percent reduced how hard they work,
- 47 percent spent less time at work,
- 66 percent saw a decline in their performance, and
- 78 percent felt less committed to the organization.[26]

Unchecked incivility is a by-product, in part, of low-quality relationships. At work, the place where we spend the bulk of our daily time, employees should not be mentally distracted worrying about their safety because of poor work relationships with colleagues.

Other human needs, such as the need for accomplishment, contributing to something bigger than one's self, and even growing as a person also reveal why work is not fulfilling for most employees. A by-product of the Industrial Era when managers treated employees as replaceable cogs in the factory's assembly line, the dehumanization of people—who are viewed merely as a necessity to make money—still lingers in corporate cultures, though it is not as overt as it was a century ago. Instead, the dehumanization occurs through subtle practices like requiring employees who work from home to complete reports showing their work progress. This method conveys to employees a management message that says, "I don't trust that you will work when you are at home. So I'll make you report what you do so that I feel better about this practice that I don't personally like."

Unfortunately, notable recent examples of overt mistreatment of employees have dominated news headlines. Uber's CEO, Travis Kalanick, had to step down from his role because of the company's unchecked bro-culture, sexism in the workplace, and claims of unethical business practices. Also, consider the sweatshop mentality that dominated Wells Fargo's sales leaders. They set impossibly aggressive sales goals. Bankers were unable to meet their goals and resorted to illegally opening accounts for customers without their consent. While these two examples are extreme, the business tactics and the outdated mindsets that design them lurk in offices across the country. It is not only customers who suffer. Employees take the brunt of the mistreatment.

Employees do not want to be at work when it is an exhausting game of "keep your head down to avoid getting pulled into office drama." When the workplace is hostile or toxic, each day employees struggle to decide if they should keep quiet when they are mistreated or speak up when they see others mistreated. In these environments, most see little progress in their work and wonder what value they contribute. Hostile and toxic work environments prevent anyone from finding fulfillment.

While creating a sense of belonging is not the only answer to the problems explained above, it is an important step forward. When you purposely create an environment people want to in, you position employees to develop meaningful relationships that help facilitate doing work that matters. Here are three compelling inputs that transform the experience of work:

1. Create a desirable work environment,
2. Have meaningful relationships, and
3. Do work that matters.

Advantage Five:
Teams Become More Cohesive

A team of people who are just acquaintances will not achieve exceptional levels of success. At work, if you only know someone casually, how willing would you be to go out of your way to help her? If you do not know someone's work ethic and skills, would you want to recruit them to help you with a high-profile project? Researchers from the University of Pennsylvania and the University of Minnesota found most workers would be hesitant. The researchers also found that teams of acquaintances underperform compared to teams with strong friendships. It turns out that when we find our place in a team we are more comfortable and willing to commit to the start of projects, maintain open communication, provide honest feedback and give praise, and we are more critical when evaluating ideas.[27] These are all invaluable inputs to high performing teams. It is unwise to underestimate the value of friendships at work. They foster frankness, compassion, understanding, even raise our expectations of one another. You create a competitive advantage by promoting belongingness.

Keith Richards once said, "When it comes to music, if we work on it together, there's something that just happens. I don't know how or why: I leave that to the mysteries of alchemy."[28] The chemistry Richards references is not limited to art and the creative process. You are a "human chemist." How you bring people and their talents together is your "alchemy." Without a bonding agent, like belonging, employees are rebels without a shared purpose. Though the Rolling Stones' lead guitarist is satisfied with not understanding "the mysteries of alchemy," I am not. *Work Tribes* examines how the hidden currents between us can be directed to influence your team's creative process, whatever that might be. I hope that in this chapter I have conveyed a sense that belonging is not some mystical or spiritual topic. Instead, I hope you will see the stories, examples, and data as inputs to a playbook for business leaders. This playbook is one that will help create an experience of work that is compelling, undeniably human, and unlocks our innate desire to be part of something bigger than our own wants and needs.

CHAPTER 2

THE FICTION
IN MANAGEMENT

The Balderdash and Beliefs That No Longer Belong in Today's Workplace

Don't accept people's resignation for mediocrity.

—Jaime Escalante

J aime Escalante, the esteemed math teacher who once taught at Garfield High School in East Los Angeles, California, rejected the stereotype that poor Hispanic students could not learn advanced mathematics. He successfully taught a group of students to pass the advance placement exam for calculus. More accurately, he helped the students pass the exam twice. The first time, the company that administered the exam rejected the students' scores. Company officials believed that the students had cheated. Their insidious belief that poor His-panic students could not possibly be smart enough to pass the test was rooted in unchallenged beliefs that minimized human potential. In this case, it was the potential of students who had been marginalized because of stereotypes and bureaucracy. However, fitting for the movie-style happy ending, the students successfully passed the exam the second time, proving they knew the material.[1]

The trivial nonsense that Jaime Escalante had to overcome also guides a preponderance of organizations today. Compa-nies and leaders who focus on petty differences—race, college GPAs, gender—or rely on unchallenged belief systems when attracting desirable and hirable employees are distracted by a meaningless conversation that is merely noise. What's worse is these companies and leaders become or remain irrelevant. The focus when hiring or retaining employees needs to be on life and work experiences, strengths, character, growth mindsets, and change agility. Belongingness will not have a transforma-tive effect on the culture when any company of any size chooses to overlook the virtues in our humanity. Following the logic in the previous statement, failing to understand human needs and their motivating influence on people is like management malpractice.

Unchallenged beliefs are what initially held back the Gar-field High School students. It was both their self-doubting beliefs and those expressed by the exam company that ensnared the teens in an unfortunate confirmation-bias conundrum. When the exam proctors initially denounced the test scores, it confirmed for the students that the system was against them, a struggle that dominated their lives.

Confirmation biases are mental shortcuts. They allow us to make quick decisions without fully examining all the facts or questioning our own thinking. Such a bias shapes our beliefs and allows them to remain unchallenged. If you believe that men are better sales people, you will overlook evidence that questions your belief. You likely will also disregard or rationalize why a contrarian belief is irrelevant. Even well-intended leaders allow bias to interfere with their conclusions. It is hard to escape their limits.

Think of changing realities as triggers for reevaluating beliefs. The trick, of course, is to observe the triggers and respond. At least at an intuitive level, most of us are aware that opinions, beliefs, and mores have changed or are changing. Consider the #MeToo movement in America. The prevailing belief system that women are inferior to men is finally being turned on its head. In business and in leadership, bias causes us to do unnecessary damage to the experience of work, the culture and climate, the company's reputation, and even our own reputations. On the human side, performance suffers, needs go unmet, employees' mental health slips, and employees' learned apathy burrows deep into their mindset. In the end trust levels erode.

From small to medium to large companies, leaders up and down the hierarchy need to reexamine their leadership beliefs. In organizations and teams where belonging is experienced, leaders are aware of how work effects their employees' lives. They express understanding and appreciation for the sacrifices employees make in support of the company's needs. Yet, when uncontested beliefs about the relationship between a business and its workers alienate one from the others in an organization, problems like low employee engagement levels, rampant distress, and a sense of feeling overwhelmed adversely affect company goals.

Something needs to change. A solid place to start is to stop being seduced by the fiction in management.

STOP BELIEVING THESE FICTITIOUS MANAGEMENT BELIEFS

Once upon a time, there was a gaggle of managers who were believed to have more knowledge than anyone in the entire land. Anyone who was not a manager acquiesced to the all-knowing bosses out of fear of losing his or her job. One day a unicorn slid down a rainbow and planted seeds. These seeds, however, were special ones. For they were Idea Seeds and they were magical. No one could see the seeds because the unicorn secretly placed them in employees' brains. With each passing day the seeds began to grow. As they grew, the non-managers started seeing the shackles that were a drag on their potential. This magical occurrence was a surprise at first. But over time the nonmanagers, and even some from the gaggle of managers, realized that they were duped. There was another choice they could make. It was a scary one, though. The nonmanagers and some of the enlightened managers secretly met out of view of the all-seeing eye that managers were believed to have. In this meeting the two groups explored a new paradigm that would challenge centuries of belief. Ultimately, these renegades adopted a new belief—businesses, people leaders (formerly managers), and employees could redefine the relationships between them and could live happily ever after. But one issue plagued their progress: How to change?

Removing my tongue from my cheek, I will stop mythologizing the history of management and get to the answer that eluded these curiosity-driven renegades (and get back to a non-fictional style of writing).

The moth-eaten beliefs that inform traditional management practices are finally showing their frailty. Fortunately, modern advancements in what evokes human potential are becoming more commonly understood. Advancements that are based on sound scientific research are wellsprings for the evolution away from fictitious management beliefs. Here are a few dangerous management beliefs and their modern corollary:

- *Money talks.* Researchers Richard Ryan and Edward Deci study what motivates adults. It turns out that money, advancement, and great benefits fail to motivate us in the long term. But autonomy, mastery, and purpose have a greater impact on human performance and potential.[2] The mindset and related actions linked to making an impact in people's lives outweighs money's motivating influences.
- *It's just a job.* The Conference Board released a study in 2018 revealing that both Gen X and millennials placed the work they do as the most important factor in what they look for in an employer. Even a company's mission ranked higher in value than total compensation. In short, meaningful work is central to igniting employee

engagement.[3] Moreover, people leaders, who already
have the greatest influence on workplace climate
(what it feels like to work in the team and company),
can more easily improve how a job is crafted for an
employee compared to working through HR red
tape on pay increases that amount to an insignificant
2 percent.

- *It's just business.* Researcher Paul Zak linked trust
  and trustworthiness to the neuropeptide oxytocin.
  Zak found that when people help each other or
  reciprocate on a kind gesture, the brain releases
  oxytocin, deepening the bond or connection between
  people. Empathetic leaders are more effective than
  commanding managers.[4] The impact a leader has
  on his people has long been dismissed as a casualty
  of "doing business." An old-school manager who is
  unaware of how his words or indecision influences
  relationships and the culture is an organizational
  weakness and a liability.

Each of the above advancements are outcomes from a proliferation of scientific inquiries. Researchers and academics
are helping us to understand what truly motivates us, captures
our commitment, and ultimately shapes our awareness of the
value of our humanity. Researchers are learning what aspects
of work-life are truly desirable to people. Advancements from
ongoing neuroscience studies are revealing what is happening
in the brain when we establish new relationships or nurture
longstanding ones. You do not need to be a psychologist to
lead people. You do, however, need to be willing to challenge

the belief that management is the most influential discipline in business.

Adults do not like to be managed. The lingering, archaic, command-and-control micromanagement styles are no longer effective. Historically speaking, management was designed to find and exploit efficiencies in factories. Its very premise was built on control and maximizing profit, which both diminish the importance of relationships and their benefits at work. Today, what motivates adults is a collaborative, affiliative style of leadership. With this style, leaders have a responsibility to help people and the business grow. This agreement is far more sustainable. When management is the predominant driver in a company, the work arrangement remains transactional and impersonal. Conversely, when effective leadership proliferates throughout the business, the work arrangement becomes relational. This is at the heart of belonging.

FIRST, THIS IS WHAT EMPLOYEES WANT

The intrinsic value of employees' talents, strengths, and ideas to employers has been commodified and exploited for the benefit of profit. The employment contract has been unchallenged for centuries even though employees' needs and expectations have evolved.

In 2017, I conducted an online poll to learn what employees wanted from their work. The question I asked was simple: What do you want from the work you do besides a paycheck? With more than two hundred responses, the answers were aspirational. In fact, most of the themes align with basic human needs like belonging.[5]

Like The Conference Board found in their research, the top "want" in my poll was to do meaningful work. Statements such as "make a contribution to society," "need a reason to get up," "help teams find a purpose," "direct my passion," and "leave a legacy" were common and had many variations in the way the sentiment was expressed.

Meaning has a profound influence on the human condition. Without meaning, the cynicism and cruelty of the world would dominate over hope and possibilities, blinding us to a full view of life. Victor Frankl wrote in *Man's Search for Meaning,* "An active life serves the purpose of giving man the opportunity to realize values in creative work, while a passive life of enjoyment affords him the opportunity to obtain fulfillment in experiencing beauty, art, or nature."[6] Meaningful work is both actively pursued and passively observed. As humans, we are roused by the notion to make something better than we found it. We are moved or inspired by what others have created. Noticers, leaders who have a developed a keen sense of observation, initiate conversations with their team members to learn what brings meaning to their work. The act of noticing also catches moments that reveal what lights up employees when they do something that energizes them. Look out for the subtle cues that point the direction to employees' strengths. They are vital inputs for leaders who want to create a sense of belonging.

Another highly desirable reality that people shared was the importance of meaningful relationships. From a cheeky (perhaps hopeful) response like, "I get away from my family and kids" to reflective statements like "to need and be needed," the myriad ways respondents expressed the role that relationships play in the experience of work breaks open the myth that we work only for a paycheck.

In a 2016 *Harvard Business Review* article, researchers found that over the past twenty years collaborative work has increased by 50 percent.[7] Employees are spending more time in teams to meet the demands of an often-crippling work pace. Also, the nature of work today relies on the knowledge each person brings to the team. No one person can single-handedly complete a project. For a business to continuously grow, adjust, and change, it must tap into the many disciplines that help create value for customers and all other stakeholders of the company. Does it not make sense, then, to remove silly impediments and challenge outmoded thinking that myopically reinforces individualism over collaborative relationships? The rapid pace of change challenges all sizes of businesses to learn how to bring diverse groups of people together. Meaningful relationships raise a team's performance and allow discovery of new ways to overcome the biases and barriers: these prevent the exploration of innovative methods that create relevant solutions.

"[I am] addicted to accomplishments," proclaimed one leader from my online poll. Another simply said, "Without accomplishing something, I would be bored [at work]." Though the first two themes were aspirational, these next two are utilitarian: feel a sense of accomplishment and be useful. Employees at all levels can become weary and apathetic, partly an outcome of disinterested or poorly skilled leaders. Yes, employees shoulder responsibility for their own success.

But when the person leading does not show empathy or have a caring nature, employees turn apathetic. To feel a sense of accomplishment and to be useful is what any human being wants. I have no doubt that there is an endless amount of work to be done in your company. For this reason alone, your employees should experience these two outcomes with great regularity.

"Multipliers are genius makers. Everyone around them gets smarter and more capable. People may not become geniuses in a traditional sense, but multipliers invoke each person's unique intelligence and create an atmosphere of genius—innovation, productive effort, and collective intelligence." These are the insightful words of Liz Wiseman from her book *Multipliers*.[8] On the surface, multiplier may sound like a leader's role. That is a false assumption. People leaders are uniquely positioned to help their teams grow individually and collectively. However, all employees, in formal and informal roles of leadership, can amplify the talents and intelligence of those with whom they work. To be a multiplier, to use Wiseman's term, is another reason people get up each workday. And it is the most unique reason people gave.

What is unique about being a multiplier is that it is mostly about other people. Yet helping others tap into their genius and watching them flourish, find meaning in their work, experience accomplishments, and feel useful is also personally gratifying. If Jaime Escalante were alive today, I would like to ask him how he felt watching his students transform into confident young adults. I suspect he would downplay his part in each of his student's lives. The beauty in being a multiplier is its quiet nature. Multipliers tend to not be boastful about their style. They believe in the human potential of each person they help and accept the responsibility to guide, challenge, and encourage. Multiplying talent is always about the other person. The benefits that flow back to the multiplier are nice perks for stepping into the leadership role.

One final theme remains in my exploration of what employees want from their work—meaningful moments. First, though, a few words of caution: Be wary of quick conclusions about the relevancy and place these positive experiences hold on us. Technology companies are notorious for their forward-thinking cultures. But do not confuse slides, pool tables, and cereal bars as important ingredients to meaningful moments at work. While none of these workplace cultural artifacts are wrong or bad, they can be misused. In toxic or bland cultures, the unifying effects of pool tables, ping-pong tables, or a wall of beer is lost. They become novelties instead of symbols of the importance of relationships, connection, and even having fun.

Meaningful moments are memorable events or gestures that leave an indelible impression and are considered special. These experiences are rarely major moments. Whether it is a compliment from a colleague, an astonishing, welcoming first day on the job, or an unexpected gesture, meaningful moments elicit positive emotions. In my poll, terms like "joy" and "freedom," were emotions people felt when recalling a positive experience at work. In the blur of a busy workday and week, standout moments that leave people feeling good shape how they view working with you and for your company. Positive perceptions of the experience of work are strongly shaped by meaningful moments—planned and spontaneous.

THE ALIENATION FROM FICTIONAL MANAGEMENT BELIEFS

The corporate playbook for responding to a scandal can often enrage customers instead of reconciling their unmet expectations. Corporate responses to a gaffe (or worse) often start with some variation of denial or an explanation, often after a company is "called out" to respond. In 2017, Apple was accused of slowing down older model iPhones with batteries that could undermine the phone's performance. Once the issue made major media outlets, the company apologized. Apparently, the issue was a "misunderstanding." However, the highly technical explanation for the phone's performance problems revealed a worse issue: Apple knew about the problem but chose not to be proactive in working with impacted customers.[9]

In the same year, United Airlines CEO Oscar Muñoz needed to make a more sincere apology after his robotic response to a viral video showing a sixty-nine-year old man being dragged down the aisle in one of the company's planes. Muñoz had characterized the passenger as "disruptive and belligerent," providing a graceless justification for bloodying the passenger's face while being forcibly removed. In both examples the responses showed a lack of respect for people and an inability to genuinely connect with the public in a human way.

Whether intended or not, Apple and United's PR strategies in these two cases follow well-worn strategies that are, unfortunately, rooted in fictional management beliefs. These beliefs only frustrate and alienate customers and employees. Their overuse has one primary aim: damage control with plausible deniability. Certainly, the long-term viability of your company is of upmost importance. However, blaming or ignoring customers, as we have seen, is no longer an acceptable response.

While the Apple and United examples are customer focused, these fictional, outdated management beliefs also dramatically influence the experience of belonging. These antiquated beliefs negatively influence public perception and cause issues for employees. I doubt United employees felt a sense of pride watching how their employer handled a customer altercation. Embarrassment or shame do not elicit pride in people. Negative emotions linked to how a company manages its reputation hurt the culture and a company's ability to create a sense of belonging.

So, what are these fictional management beliefs? There are three categories of belief systems: company-centric beliefs, transactional beliefs, and in-exchange beliefs. Each belief system drives how a company and its leaders interact with all stakeholders.

Company-centric beliefs solely benefit the business. The beliefs, which can go unspoken and are modeled and followed based on unchallenged tribal knowledge—"It's how we do things here"—drive managers to make decisions that generate value only for the company. An example of a common company-centric belief is daily travel and entertainment per diems. A major corporation in the United States that shall remain nameless has a blanket travel meal per diem for all employees. An employee traveling to the Midwest has an eighteen dollar meal allowance. Employees traveling to New York City are held to the same per diem. There is nothing wrong with fiscal conservatism. At the same time, the employees I talked with tell me they feel as though it's assumed they wouldn't make smart choices. With this example, the company-centric belief is that employees are unable to make appropriate dining decisions. In the end, it's management who knows best.

Transactional beliefs depersonalize employment by viewing a job as an exchange of time for money. The primary driver behind this set of beliefs is maximum utility for the business.

- "It would benefit the company if you did not spend company time dealing with personal matters."
- "I'll hire someone of color to represent the diversity of our customer-base."
- "We do roll call for all phone meetings to make sure everyone hears the same message at the same time."

If you added, "I don't trust you, so . . ." in front of each bullet, the dehumanization of employment becomes familiar and clear. In contrast, companies that look at the experience employees have while at work possess a mutually beneficial set of beliefs:

- "We provide access to medical professionals when employees need to care for elderly parents."
- "Our managers are expected to have a mentor who is two levels above their current role."

- "Employees are adults. Therefore, we openly share issues that are hindering growth. We need to hear divergent ideas that haven't been considered."

Finally, *loyalty beliefs* shape how the company and its managers prioritize the development of the workforce. Often, complaints like, "I don't want to train people because they just leave" limit a team's performance, and managers appear out of touch. Managers also myopically focus on improving employee weaknesses. There is little awareness of the value of leveraging employees' strengths—the type of work that energizes employees and that they are good at or show great potential in mastering.

Managers are people. So it is completely reasonable that they would fall into a rut. Ruts are convenient. Seductive. Predictable. Simultaneously, ruts are excuses for adapting to changing needs and expectations. Fictional management beliefs are a set of ruts that undermine personal credibility. They also interfere with team agility—changing when needed to accomplish great outcomes.

A SHIFT IN BELIEFS

The opposite of fictional management beliefs are human-centered leadership beliefs. On the whole, these beliefs emphasize mutuality and prioritize relationships as a way to achieve success. And given that these beliefs exist in a business context, high performance expectations dominate.

In Seattle, Washington, a third-generation fine-dining restaurant epitomizes human-centered leadership beliefs. At Canlis, the restaurant's mission is to turn people toward each other. It is an unusual mission for a restaurant, but it is the heart and soul of how the restaurant is run. And it also significantly influences how every employee—from the back office, to the kitchen, to the bartenders, to the servers—interacts with one another and guests.

Canlis, ranked as one of the top-twenty best restaurants in America, is the winner of numerous Wine Spectator Grand Awards, and in 2017 it won the James Beard Outstanding Wine Program award. The industry recognition is evidence for how well the Canlis team works together. Even effusive praise from the *New York Times* recognizes the accomplishments of the nearly-seventy-years-old restaurant.

With my research partner, I visited Canlis, with its beautiful views of Lake Washington. Our mission was to understand how the restaurant was leveraging human-centered leadership beliefs to achieve such prestigious accolades. Through interviews, observations, and even tasting the Japanese-influenced creations of head chef Brady Williams, we learned firsthand what makes Canlis stand out as a workplace shaped by a sense of belonging.

Paramount to the Canlis culture are meaningful moments or experiences. Each night every employee knows exactly what and why each guest is celebrating at the restaurant. For now, I want to look at how the absence of fictional management beliefs clears the way for belonging to emerge. A little later in the book I will show you how Canlis applies human-centered leadership beliefs to powerfully shape not only the customer experience but the employees' experience.

First, rather than the beliefs that emphasize value creation benefiting the company only, human-centered beliefs emphasize a stakeholder approach. For example, at Canlis, vendor relationships are collaboratively built, demonstrating the owner's long history of finding win-win-wins for all business partners. When vendor relationships are built on trust, it is far easier to grow together as opposed to transactional interactions that emphasize a one-sided relationship. Stakeholder beliefs put a premium on building relationships centered on shared and respected values. Additionally, the mission or purpose colors how employees, owners, shareholders, vendors, and customers experience the company's offerings, products, and services. Values and purpose create consistency. These two determine how decisions are made.

You may be thinking that values and purpose are well-known workplace heavyweights. "What's so different about them?" you may wonder. Their influence is pronounced in companies that diligently embody living values and an internalized and personalized purpose. At Canlis, three values shape the employees' experience of work: trustworthiness, generosity, and other-centeredness. These guide how experiences are delivered when guests arrive for their special night. The company's mission and values shape everything from how the reservation is taken, how complaints are handled, and even the high expectations on every employee. "[We] expect employees to speak up for themselves," explains Katie Hoffman, Canlis's Director of Operations.[10] To pull off a night full of experiences—a wedding proposal, a ninety-fourth-birthday celebration—every employee must know their part and all details tended to with diligence.

A stakeholder belief structure works to unify relationships and create a sense of community. Another benefit from the human-centered leadership beliefs is how valued employees feel. This category of belief system, other-focused, emphasizes interactions that benefit the company and employees. Other-focused beliefs signal that the company understands how work impacts employees' lives. For example, Nelson Daquip, who is Canlis's Director of Wine and Spirits and an Advanced Sommelier, was given time off to study for the Master Sommelier exam. The exam is incredibly difficult, and Daquip had been working long hours leading his team and managing his portion of the business, leaving little time to study. Mark and Brian Canlis, the owners of the restaurant, did not hesitate to suggest Daquip take a paid sabbatical to prepare. When a company-centric belief dominates the culture, flexible and supportive actions to support employees are absent. Managers are not encouraged to think about or evaluate alternative ways to support employee success. This can perpetuate a belief that employees' needs are secondary to the company's success. At Canlis, a focus on what Daquip needed will benefit customers and the business while deepening the future Master Sommelier's pride for and commitment to the restaurant.

In Table 2.1, the final belief system listed in the human-centered leadership column is learning. Where the fictional management set of beliefs views training as a reward for select high performers, more evolved companies view learning new skills as an unending series of investments. All employees are required to be willing to engage in unending wisdom-loops: learning new skills that lead to growth that lead to deeper learning.

TABLE 2.I: BELIEF SYSTEMS COMPARISON CHART

Fictional Management Beliefs	Human-Centered Leadership Beliefs
Company-Centric Beliefs *Beliefs that place the company as the beneficiary of its value-creation activities.* • Profit is our purpose • Hire people who "fit" the culture • What gets measured gets managed • Pay is recognition for doing your job • Management knows best • Short-term view • You work for the company (one-sided)	**Stakeholder Beliefs** *Beliefs that place primary importance on those who benefit from the company's value-generation activities.* • Purpose is the North Star • Hire people who complement and advance the culture • Measure what shapes and promotes high performance • Culture of feedback and recognition • Gauging readiness for change • Balance long- and short-term objectives • Promote organizational community
One-Sided Beliefs *Emphasis on hiring employees to support the needs of the company.* • Separate your personal life from your professional one • Differences benefit the company • Friends at work are a distraction • Employees need to be controlled and monitored or they will slack off	**Others-Focused Beliefs** *Emphasis on partnering with employees to achieve mutually beneficial outcomes.* • Whole-person perspective • Evaluate the well-being of stakeholder relationships when making changes • Proactive mindset to leverage diversity benefits • Build high-quality relationships • Use transparency and consistency to build trust with employees
Growth Beliefs *Beliefs that shape how managers prioritize who gets trained.* • Myopic focus on weaknesses • Promote individual performance • Be well-rounded • Training is a benefit or reward	**Learning** *Emphasis on required ongoing learning to mitigate and close skill gaps.* • Align work with strengths • Reward and recognize teams and individuals • Develop team agility • Require staying in wisdom-loops • Promote coaching and mentoring

In a 2018 IBM study, chief human resource officers (CHROs) were asked about their talent management needs. In the context of rapid technological advancements, business-model disruptions, and ongoing change, CHROs expressed concerns that existing employees and people leaders need a deeper skill set related to working in teams. In short, people skills are in high demand; 61 percent of CHROs placed inter- and intrapersonal skills as a top need.[11]

The twentieth-century management belief upholding employment as a transaction may never go away. It will, however, be an anchor holding back progress. The game of business has changed. A more meaningful employment exchange has replaced the old psychological contract; it is now relational. The three categories of beliefs for human-centered leadership view working together as a reciprocity of sentiments. The positive nature imbued in the sentiments is powerful enough for any organization to reach an esteemed status in employees' minds. This has nothing to do with a "you scratch my back and I'll scratch yours" mentality. Today work can be a source of bone-deep pride that unifies a team of people who want to feel the joys of their hard work.

The next question is how do you lead people so that they know their contribution (effort and sacrifice) is valued? That the sum of their experiences, how they think, and the strengths and skills they have are wanted? And the ultimate test: How welcomed do people feel in your company? In your team? When we feel welcomed we can settle in and be at ease in our environment and with our colleagues . . . friends. We can get on with doing our best work.

CHAPTER 3

THE EXPERIENCE OF BELONGING

A Personal Revolution in How Your Lead

We can believe what we choose. We are answerable for what we choose to believe.

—Cardinal John Henry Newman

L et's play a game. It will be quick; I promise. The rules are simple. To start, first read the below scenario.

Two men in the military are hanging out and talking. Man 1 asks Man 2 if he would trade patrol assignments with him. Though the trade would benefit the second man, he declines.

45

Now choose the best reason for Man 2 to decline trading patrol assignments:

A. He doesn't like Man 1.
B. He doesn't trust Man 1.
C. He's worried about breaking protocol.
D. None of the above.

This game is an experiment Daniel Kahneman and his research partner, Amos Tversky, designed to study how the possibility of a loss will bias our decisions.[1] A natural response any of us have to loss is to prevent the associated feelings from happening in the first place. Look carefully at the four options in the game. The first three center on whom? Man 2. So to avoid the possibility of feeling regret and the loss of a brother, the best option is *D*—none of the above. The fourth option frees you from making a judgment call about the other soldier's character or likability. It also positions you to avoid negative emotions. After all, if soldiers swap shifts and the one who stays on duty is killed (sorry to be so morbid), the one who did not work will likely feel a deep sense of regret.

Regret, it turns out, is a significant influence on the decisions we make.

If you are unfamiliar with Kahneman, he was awarded the 2002 Nobel Prize based on his joint work with Tversky. A significant theme in their work is that humans are not as logical as we like to believe. Backed by mounds of compelling, well-designed research, the findings are quite contrarian in the field of economics. The truth is, we humans are inclined to many types of bias that cloud our thinking, judgment, and ultimately our decisions.

Choice. Choose. Choosing. Decide. Decision. No matter the word you prefer, the outcome is still the same: one thing wins over another, unless you choose not to make a choice. It is the distinction of choice that brings us to the next exploration of belonging. I present to choose or not to choose. For a moment I want to bring you out of the passive role of the reader and into the active role of a leader. You have a choice to make that is as powerful as the one in the Kahneman and Tversky experiment. Though a physical death is not likely to occur, a metaphorical death is. I will ask you to kill off two of three choices. The choice I will present could have regret linked to it. The good news: the other possibility is an experience that could be deeply satisfying and fulfilling.

Each day you work there is an opportunity to choose how you "up your leadership game."

Choice is not about freewill, though it is often synonymous with expressing one's individuality. "I choose what's important to me." "I decide what is best for my children." For most Americans, the primary criteria for making a choice are personal implications and the influence it might have on one's situation. Yet in other countries choice is grounded in community and harmony. "What is the best option for our neighborhood?" "What is the most appropriate choice for the greater good of the team?" Whichever definition of *choice* you believe, you are answerable for the outcomes.

In the context of the workplace and your impact on its culture and climate, the choice to facilitate a sense of belonging must be made with the greater good in mind. Which, by the way, does include your place in that greater good. But as Mark and Brian Canlis shared with me, "If you want to create a sense of belonging, do so with clarity and intention."[2] I would add that the intention must be well-meaning, purposeful, and for the greater good. Without showing employees why belonging is important and what you are willing to do to encourage it, you risk creating another management fad: "She's only doing 'this' because she read a new leadership book. We'll see how long 'this one' will last."

The choices I present to you are straightforward:

1. Choose to take on the challenge of facilitating a sense of belongingness at work
2. Choose to not take on the challenge of facilitating belongingness at work
3. Choose to not make a choice

Before you choose, let me continue to level with you. Adopting the leadership practices listed in this chapter is wholly about people *and* performance. Your efforts will stall or fail if the focus is on people *or* performance. A singular focus on people will alienate those who want to do great work; being nice, in this myopic view, outweighs performance without accountability. This can be dangerous. An unbalanced view biased toward how people feel and think becomes too much of a good thing. This creates what I call the country club effect. People are hanging out, having fun, and socializing, but little meaningful, important work is getting done.

As for performance, guard against a singular focus on what employees achieve or fail to achieve. When leaders signal that performance is all that matters, it will alienate employees. It reinforces the transactional view of work—exchange of time for money. Think Janet Jackson: "What have you done for me lately?" Ultimately, to genuinely show employees that they are valued, wanted, and welcomed, pair your expectations of high performance with a caring mindset. I will get into what this looks like later in this chapter. For now, remember that to uphold a sense of belonging it absolutely must be coupled with expectations of high performance. At the same time, employees and teams must learn how to depend on one another to reach high levels of success. All great achievements have more than one set of fingerprints on them.

I am sounding the alarm bells because I want you to successfully transform how your employees relate to their work and each other. By bringing belonging into your workplace, you are making a public pronouncement. Therefore, it pays to be judicious in the choice I presented to you: to bring belonging to your workplace or not. Evaluate your choice mindfully. To help you choose, spend time thinking about or writing your answers to the following questions:

- How might your culture change when employees believe they are valued, wanted, and welcomed?
- What are the implications if employees do not believe they are valued, wanted, and welcomed?
- Consider the implications to Desire, Hire, and Fire: How desirable does your organization appear to potential new hires or how desirable is it to work on your team? If you don't have a good reputation, hiring highly talented people will be difficult. Finally, when people are fired or leave, the quality of the relationship

will make it easier or more complicated, even litigious.

- When your employees feel valued, wanted, and welcomed, how do your stakeholders benefit: customers, employees, teams, management, the board?
- How would a sense of belonging add to your personal fulfillment at work?

There is a pernicious belief I often hear managers articulate: "I don't have time for this stuff." Sure, creating a positive workplace and meeting with employees takes time. But the reality is that weak relationships take up more time: dealing with underperformance and the related HR paperwork, refereeing workplace drama, chasing solutions to high turnover, even dealing with disappointment from a lack of innovative ideas.

Greatness cannot emerge when people don't care.

A PLACE WHERE PEOPLE WANT TO BE

"It's bullshit." Doug Conant cried foul on the flippant belief "It's not personal; it's business." Conant, the storied CEO who led the turnaround of Campbell Soup Company, holds firmly that business must be personal. "Nothing of significance is accomplished when people don't care," he told me.[3] When employees choose to invest their time in your company, it is absolutely a personal matter. After all, they are investing on average nearly six full days of work a week. The casual denial of the sacrifice employees make responding to emails after hours, or staying late and missing another family event because of a last-minute work deadline *is* personal. The belief that bothers Conant underscores the icy tolerance of impersonal interactions at work.

We have entered a time where companies cannot risk the damage to their reputations when managers behave as if they are set apart from everyone else. After all, these managers are merely one step away from an unsatisfied employee's Facebook confessional. Crappy managers also need to be prepared to serve as the inspiration for a harsh review on Glassdoor. Glassdoor, a cheeky metaphor for transparency, is a job site that allows current and former employees to rate a company and its management. When underperforming managers are allowed to underwhelm, the site acts as a megaphone for employees to expound on the quality of a company's culture and even the effectiveness of the CEO. Dismiss the input at your peril. Perhaps the truth may be somewhat skewed (or not), but the perceptions of you and your company are real. And when these perceptions work against you and your company, you have a place of employment where people do not want to be.

Doug Conant can tell you what happens when managers and companies lose their way, their identity—or worse. Companies that fail to exemplify who they say they are appear fraudulently, untrustworthy.

In 2002, Conant took on the daunting responsibility of bringing Campbell's back from its slide into irrelevancy. It would have been predictable to pay millions of dollars for an ad campaign reestablishing the iconic brand's presence in consumers' lives. Conant, however, knew that to win in the marketplace, Campbell's had to win in the workplace. His decision to focus inward was deeply aligned with the company's purpose. It also aligned with a deeply human-centered mindset.

As Conant and his direct leadership team plotted the soup company's turnaround, a clear focus guided their decisions and actions. Before I analyze the approach of this well-documented comeback, a little context is needed. First, in the time preceding Conant's appointment as CEO, Campbell's had lost half its market share in one year. Imagine if you lost half of your financial value in a year. That would be unsettling, right? Next, employees were deeply dissatisfied and disillusioned. Campbell's had the worst engagement levels among all of the *Fortune* 500 companies. In Camden, New Jersey, where the company headquarters are located, employees did not feel safe. To sum up, Campbell's was in trouble financially, and employees both did not want to be at work and worried about their safety going to and from work.

Major corporations are notorious for their short-term perspective. In other words, enacting changes that give the balance sheet a needed nudge—which in turn satisfy shareholders and the market—is often rule one in a comeback strategy. For Conant and his team, that hackneyed strategy was not an option. Instead, the focus was on creating a place where associates and people leaders wanted to be and stay.

What I find delicious about this vision is the symbolism in using Campbell's core-value proposition—food. Food is a powerful way to connect people together. From hilarious to life changing, conversations over food have transformed relationships. Food is tradition. It is enriched by stories. Part of the human experience is to enjoy a meal with family and friends. The union over food is what helped bring employees together and reinvigorate Campbell's.

RETHINK: INITIATE YOUR PERSONAL LEADERSHIP REVOLUTION

What exactly did Conant help facilitate at Campbell's? His approach serves as a model for rethinking how you view leadership and its impact on you, your team, and your company.

Leadership is not a role but an orientation. The word orientation has insightful definitions that are central to rethinking leadership:

1. A person's awareness of self with regard to position and time and place and personal relationships.
2. An integrated set of values and beliefs.

Combine the two definitions above, and you now have a much more powerful view of leadership: Your self-awareness and your place in the organization shape the relationships you develop, and they are governed by your values and beliefs. Values are your operating system. Beliefs are what you maintain to be true about yourself and others. Conant was painfully aware that 19,655 employees were suffering under poor leadership. To motivate them to understand the severity of Campbell's dysfunctional relationships, they needed a new leadership orientation.

The starting place: implementing a radical rethinking of Campbell's culture. It began with connection, or what I call "Legacy and Fingerprints." Legacy and Fingerprints begins by asking people what impact they want to have on the company and inviting them to shape and implement solutions linked to that impact they view as important. At Campbell's, this meant asking employees how connected they felt to the company. Once the areas of disconnection were identified, six hundred work groups across the company formed to change the culture. It was a data-driven process, and managers were held accountable to show support for the changes and employee involvement.[4]

Naturally with this sort of rethinking, people opted out and left. Three hundred leaders left during Campbell's reset period. As managers left, employee engagement went up.[5] A profound impact on engagement happened after the company began reinvesting in the Camden, New Jersey, community. Remember, employees did not feel safe in the area. So to help improve safety, Campbell's turned to what it is good at, making nutritious food, as a way to improve the surrounding community. The strategy was to invest in the community's youth by giving them access to healthy food, expanding on programs that promoted physical activity, and educating young children on the importance of healthy snacks. It was a $10 million investment over a ten-year period aiming to reduce childhood obesity by 50 percent.[6] The outcome was that employees felt a deep sense of pride and fulfillment working for the soup company. It took years for the storied company to win back the hearts and hands of its employees, creating a place they wanted to be and stay.[7]

LEADER ROLE VERSUS LEADER ORIENTATION

The clearer your leader orientation, the more significant your contributions become. The differences between a leader-role and a leader-orientation mindset are subtle and understanding them is essential to belonging. The leader-role mindset is shaped by hierarchy, a common human way to make sense of relationships. This mindset bases actions and decisions on the power imbued in his or her role. Each leader has his or her swim lane and does not swim across the lane lines. Risk aversion is often high. Maintaining stability is the goal with those who stay in their lane. Even in nature hierarchy is assumed. Hens and chickens maintain a rigid hierarchy, with the most senior hens roosting above all other hens and chickens in the pen. As for humans, evolutionary psychology shows that we, too, automatically tier relationships and infer types of power to one's place and role in social situations. Yet, hierarchy can add drag to progress, making it a liability if it is not used appropriately. Or, as the cliché goes, not everything is a nail when you're the hammer.

A leader-orientation mindset does not disregard the hierarchy. Instead, the orientation is around performance and uses the hierarchy to make sense of how to navigate the company to accelerate growth and progress. In contrast to the leader-role mindset, risk-taking is more encouraged as a necessity to guide a team to greatness, though it does not mean that risks are taken lightly. Unlike the rigidity of hierarchy, a performance-driven mindset pushes leaders to seek out people and resources to meet or exceed goals. High-quality relationships become the currency that makes leader orientation stand out compared to role-based leadership.

One final comparison is necessary between the two belief systems. I turn to Dr. David Sirota, workplace researcher and consultant and author, for the final point on this topic: "The point of leadership is not the status that can come with it, but the contribution the person makes. In companies around the world, management has become the position (role) many want. It is like a trophy for a hard-won fight. No manager should be in the role if he or she is not interested in coaching or mentoring people. Equally as important is the desire to continue to learn and grow. A colleague once said, 'If you're green you're growing; if you're ripe you're rotting.'"[8]

The orientation of a leader accepts the mantle of responsibility to guide, grow, and expect the full-out effort from others. The responsibilities and duties associated with your leadership include showing everyone that they belong in your team or company. In the following sections, I lay out the practices that lead to belonging.

REWIRED: CHANGE UP HOW YOU SHOW UP

Canlis Restaurant is set above Lake Washington in Seattle. The fine dining restaurant features a daring, delicious menu, the artistry of Executive Chef Brady Williams. Williams is no stranger to working in high-performing, high-pressure environments. He was the executive sous chef at two different two-Michelin-star restaurants in New York: Blanca and Roberta's. Working in a kitchen is tough. Watch episodes of *Iron Chef* and you can see the pressure. So it is quite impressive that a young executive chef at one of the best restaurants in the United States, a chef at the top of his game, is fully aware of how he shows up.

When Mark and Brian Canlis interviewed Williams for the executive chef position, the process mirrored the restaurant's culture. (A better way to characterize the interview was as an experience.) At the heart of the interview design was learning how Williams interacted with staff. Mark and Brian needed to observe how he gave direction, took feedback, and responded to mistakes while he prepared a meal. Another component of the interview experience involved sitting down for a meal with Mark, Brian, and their parents, Alice and Chris Canlis. Williams was asked to critique the food served, including sharing what dish he liked least.[9]

We know the end of the story. Chef Brady aced the interview and was invited to be part of the Canlis history. If he was not gifted at his craft, he would never have been invited to an interview. However, it was Williams's ability to show grace and grit that helped him become the sixth executive chef of Canlis.

Chef Brady was more than just a fit for the Canlis culture. The popular Wharton professor and celebrity author Adam Grant uses a more appropriate term: cultural contribution.[10] When you hire new people, stop looking for fit. If fitting in has nothing to do with belonging, it has no place in hiring someone to fit into your culture. Fitting in equals falling in line. Instead, hire people who can contribute to the culture. That contribution must support the direction of your company, the evolution of your team, and the complimenting and balancing of strengths, experiences, and ways of thinking among employees.

There are nuances to leader orientation. It takes an authentic commitment to show up ready to make a difference in your employees' lives and for your customers, internal and external. Belonging will not emerge otherwise. The most powerful way to support yourself in assuming the mantle of responsibility is to surround yourself with people playing big like you.

When I interviewed Katie Coffman, Canlis's director of operations, she shared a beautiful example that shows the commitment all people leaders need to support them to show up each day ready to be at their best. Coffman and Chef Brady need to work closely together to support the Canlis team. At Canlis, their relationship is paramount to their success. So naturally the two leaders know about one another's personal lives. "I know what it's like in [Chef Brady's] personal life. When he's not able to show-up, my desire to show up for him is important [for our success] and vice versa."[11]

In case you are wondering, showing up does not mean being physically present. It is being physically, mentally, and emotionally present. The give and take nature of the support Coffman describes is a characteristic of astonishingly great teams. However, not showing up does not preclude you from radical candor: "You're not showing up right now; what's going on?" Lead with curiosity, not an accusation. The goal is to hear your team member and then work together to find a way for him to be present.

THE BELONGING PRACTICES AND THEIR ACTIONS

Cultural contribution is a fantastic example of how businesses and their leaders are evolving and becoming more human-centered. My research partner, Bruce Elliot, and I studied four model companies in different industries and sizes: The Container Store, Canlis Restaurant, LinkedIn, and Barry-Wehmiller. Each company was selected because of its well-documented, positive workplace cultures and climates.

Equally important, these companies needed to be successful in the marketplace. We talked with CEOs, senior leaders, and individual contributors. Our primary objective was to learn what it takes for a company and its people to design belonging into the experience of work. We also sought to learn the impact that belonging at work has on people and performance. From our research the following three practices emerged.

1. Be a Noticer

In companies and teams where belonging is experienced, people prioritize healthy relationships by observing what is important to their colleagues. A noticer will make small gestures to show their level of respect and depth of caring for others. The art of noticing is a small act of kindness in response to a subtle cue of what is important or of interest to a colleague. When Bruce and I arrived at Canlis for a day of interviews with employees, Amy Wong, Chef Brady's assistant, had taken careful preparations to ensure water was in every interview room, the doors had signs indicating an important conversation was underway, and even that breakfast was available.

2. Jell with Others

In the context of a workplace, jelling with others is honoring a code of conduct that contributes to an unflagging vitality in relationships. Over and over in our interviews, Bruce and I heard stories of employees purposefully finding ways to connect and strengthen their connections with others. The "belonging actions" for this practice, shown in Table 3.1, have two categories: giving and sustaining. Giving behaviors strengthen the team's bond. These behaviors guide how you connect with and understand others in productive ways. Sustaining behaviors show your commitment to continuously deepen awareness of your own quirks, talents, strengths, and even bad habits. A team's health is a composite of group dynamics shaped by the depth of each person's level of self-awareness. A team that can quickly learn from a disappointment will jell more deeply compared to a group of people who blame and deny responsibility. Shift happens. Discuss it and move on.

3. Do the Work

In American football, the flea flicker is one of my favorite plays. It happens so rarely, and it is fun to watch the defense scramble to adjust to the surprise. The play goes like this: The quarterback yells some version of "Hike!" He then laterally passes the ball to the running back. As the offense begins to chase the running back, their attention is no longer on the quarterback. Before the running back crosses the line of scrimmage, he laterally passes the ball back to the quarterback. The flick back to the quarterback, who now has less coverage, gives him a bigger window of time to find an open receiver. For the trick play to work, all offensive players must know how to set up on the line of scrimmage. If they have not invested time studying their playbook, the play will likely become a fumble. This is what "do the work" is about. Every team player does his or her part to help the team achieve success. The belonging actions for this practice keep the team focused and moving forward together. Quite simply, "Do the work" is about investing the time and being committed to creating astonishing outcomes.

TABLE 3.I: BELONGING PRACTICES

Belonging Practice	Belonging Actions What's valued to uphold the architecture of belonging
Be a Noticer A commitment to making the team's health the top priority	• Seek out and learn from different perspectives • Replace accusations with curiosity • Observe subtle queues • Develop a habit of reflection
Jell with Others A code of conduct that adds to an unflagging vitality in relationships	Giving • Show vulnerability • Express empathy • Care • Play/have fun Sustaining • Self-awareness • Self-leadership • Self-care
Do the Work Model and expect high performance	"Connect to Be Direct" • Quickly "clean up" relationship messes • Discuss purpose regularly • Focus on what's possible • Constantly create clarity

RENEW: INVIGORATE YOUR PERSONAL LEADERSHIP REVOLUTION

Table 3.1 lists the actions that contribute to team cohesion. When it comes to a workplace that leaves employees feeling valued, wanted, and welcomed, quality *and* quantity matters. Consider this for a moment: As the people leader, when you model the practices but the team does not, what outcome do you think emerges? You will likely burnout, grow frustrated, or worse, become indifferent or disillusioned. Unlike other leadership books, the actions listed on Table 3.1 are not only for managers. A culture colored by a stable and palpable sense of belonging is a result of people throughout the company practicing them.

You can probably predict what I am going to say next; you, as the people leader, are responsible for modeling the actions. Not perfectly. You are human, after all. But if you want to bring belonging to your team or company, you, the leader, must go first.

The encouraging reality about these practices is their invigorating influence on work and how you lead people. When you can tap into the deeply human phenomena of belonging, the positive emotions you experience become contagious. The contagion acts as a cultural wildfire.

Barbara Fredrickson, the Kenan Distinguished Professor of psychology at Chapel Hill University, North Carolina, has done extensive research on the contagion that spreads from person to person as a result of positive emotions. A leader's positive emotions have been found to help with workplace transformations. For example, Fredrickson's research found that when people feel safe at and satisfied with work, they are primed to experience positivity. Let's link Fredrickson's insights with the experience of belonging. Employees will feel safe and satisfied when you integrate belonging actions that shape how you relate to them. This leads to what Fredrickson calls "optimal functioning and well-being." The feel-good factor improves cognitive thinking and creativity, while helping us better respond to stress and setbacks. In the end, a virtuous cycle envelops more people as you focus on renewing how you lead and creating a place where people feel valued, wanted, and welcomed. Such a workplace is one talented people search for and want to join.

AN UNFORGETTABLE EXPERIENCE

Remember Amy Wong? She is Chef Brady's assistant at Canlis Restaurant. In my interview with Amy, she shared an invaluable work lesson she learned at the restaurant: "I can't depend on my teammates if I don't know what's going on with them or if a teammate, for some reason this week, is feeling down and not getting work done. If I know what's going on in [my colleague's] life, and if I can connect with that person. . . . then I can help them."[12]

Here is what stands out to me in Amy's words. When employees know one another, it is easier to notice when something is "off" with a colleague. Then it is not an intrusive act to inquire how a teammate is doing. The compassion for the person and the commitment to doing great work requires that we check in with one another. At Canlis, where the customer experience is their differentiator and is backed by a genuine interest in high-quality human relationships, to refrain from talking with a colleague who is underperforming jeopardizes everything that is unique about their culture. It is much easier to avoid conversations that matter because they are uncomfortable. But an unforgettable work experience is built on a caring about one another and upholding the purpose and priority of the work. Not having the difficult conversations with teammates allows mediocre performances to become the norm. Mediocre performances are not tolerated for long in teams or companies with high belongingness. Why? Because what unites teams is the bone-deep pride that comes from knowing you and your colleagues are doing great work . . . together. Anything that jeopardizes those positive emotions and progress in the work are seen as setbacks and quickly resolved.

PART II

THE HARD THINGS ABOUT SOFT THINGS

CHAPTER 4

THE OUTSIDERS

The Insidious Influence
of Indifference

*And action is the only remedy to indifference, the most
insidious danger of all.*

—Elie Wiesel

The dust kicked up by horses and carriages hung in the air. Men, hungover and fueled with a greed for gold, rushed in and out of stores buying supplies for another day of panning. It was 1869. Amid the chaos and violence of the gold rush era, twenty-two Japanese samurai, a young girl—Okei Ito—and other Japanese refugees established a farm in Coloma, California. These political refugees from Japan were no strangers to violence. It was, after all, what

67

caused them to flee their homeland; civil war was tearing apart Japan. Strangers to a new culture and landscape, I imagine the settlers felt a confusing mix of sadness for their losses, encouragement from a new beginning, and curiosity at how the Euro-Americans acted. Certainly, the cultural contrasts were significant: American gunslingers versus samurai with significant battle training and a deep respect for honor and tradition.

For the Japanese settlers, adjusting to a foreign country was not easy. Though they had some modicum of success selling what they harvested, the samurai were not gifted farmers. Predictably, they were not welcomed into the area. Their physical appearance reminded the white settlers of the Chinese residents, who were also unwelcome. A reporter for the *San Francisco Daily Morning Call* compared the samurai settlers to the Chinese residents, calling them dangerous and subhuman.

The Wakamatsu Tea and Silk Colony—the samurai's settlement—lasted two years. Because of betrayal, racism, and heartache, the settlers eventually disbanded. It is not known what happened to the Japanese colonists except for one: Okei Ito. The nursemaid stayed, waiting for the father of the family she worked for to return. He never did. Okei Ito died waiting. History does not know what happened to Okei Ito's family. Today the Wakamatsu Tea and Silk Colony is a national landmark and the resting place for the young nursemaid.[1]

What happens when we are rejected by others? The pain, as you will learn in this chapter, is physical. Imagine the profound heartbreak Okei Ito felt when her family never returned for her.

She lived as a young woman in a country that did not want her or understand her. Okei Ito and the first American Japanese settlers were not welcomed.

No matter the social context—your personal life or your professional life—to feel unwelcome is to feel a denial of your identity. As my mother-in-law, Mary Rose, once worried when we placed her into a care facility, "They don't know who I loved." She did not want to be away from our family. In a new environment our brain is hyperaware of possible threats. In the absence of a genuine, welcoming gesture, we feel unsettled, out of place, unwanted.

In the workplace, worries of acceptance, finding our way, and making friends occupy our thoughts. Like the samurai experienced, we categorize people to quickly determine who they are. We are good at fitting in.

But fitting in has no value to belonging. Revered author, speaker, and professor Brené Brown summarizes fitting in this way, as described by eighth-grade students: "[It's] being somewhere where you want to be, but they don't care one way or the other. . . . Fitting in is being accepted for being like everyone else. . . . If I have to be like you, I fit in."[2] If your middle school experience was anything like mine, fitting in meant not making eye contact with John the Bully. Fitting in was pretending to be whatever seemed to best make you blend in. Sure, people saw your physical presence. But as my mother-in-law noted, when you seek to fit in, your story is never truly known.

When employees learn to fit in, their critical and creative thinking is crippled. They learn to wait for or rely on social cues to dictate how they should think, which ideas to accept, or when to speak up, assuming such behavior is fitting within the culture. In these environments, employees waste more time worrying about how to play the game than caring about doing great work.

If your expectations are to make meaningful progress in your strategic efforts or just get the day-to-day work finished, it's time to double down on developing your leaders. Disruption from high turnover or poor manager performance causes organizational drag. The drag grows so heavy that it becomes impossible to get the momentum needed to achieve astonishing results. Yes, culture is important. It is, however, your managers' skill sets that will amplify the great parts or the ugly truths of working for your company. You have to start somewhere to create a sense of belonging. It begins with your leaders and their abilities to inspire and motivate people, as well as manage a workload that matters to the company and its stakeholders.

When employees learn to participate in the company as outsiders, leaders cannot create a workplace where differences are maximized. Instead, the nemesis of belonging poisons the culture—indifference. Where belonging leaves people feeling valued, wanted, and welcomed, indifference burrows into the hearts and minds of employees. The result is an overt and covert game to aggressively protect oneself from feeling too much. It drains our motivation to contribute. It can get uglier too. Employees who feel indifference learn not to care about the team's success and may believe that it doesn't matter that they don't care. Indifference and fitting in distract teams from bonding, performing, and respecting and admiring differences.

AS THE SAYING GOES,
BIRDS OF A FEATHER . . .

In nature, the starling birds baffle the scientific community. Starlings fly together in groups of thousands. It is not the numbers that stumps scientists, however. En masse, the small birds move together in unison, a beautifully choreographed fluidity called *murmuration*. The starlings shift left together, then right, then turn inwards, and then shift upwards, all in synchronicity. If you do not know what I'm talking about, search on YouTube for "murmuration."

What we do not know about this poetic aerial display of movement is why or how the birds move together. One of the prevailing theories is that it is a survival tactic. Starling birds are small, making them easy prey for larger birds. Perhaps strength in numbers and rapid movements make the birds more difficult to hunt? One theory that seems to hold true across many scientific studies is that murmurations are biologically driven. They are a form of communication, which spreads like information in a network. Birds interact with others around them, six or seven to be exact. Imagine a wave of awareness about an impending hawk attack rapidly spreading through the sets of bird "friends," if you will. The synchronicity of behavior helps the starling flock survive.

A similar phenomenon exists in humans, albeit its visibility is much more nuanced, if not imperceptible. It is called *neural synchrony*. Sure, the term is not as poetic as murmurations, but at least it has a loose similarity to the name of one of the best albums from the rock band The Police. Joking aside, neural synchrony has a powerful, performance-enhancing value. It also strengthens ties between people, enriching relationships—even those at work. Unfortunately, indifference can negate the positive effects of neural synchrony. What do I mean by indifference? What exactly is neural synchrony? And what does this have to do with employees finding a sense of belonging at work? Let me show you.

ENDLESSLY FASCINATED BY PEOPLE LIKE YOU

The hard thing about soft things is not their invisibility. Sure, it is difficult to resolve conflict when you may not know one exists in the first place. What makes the soft things so damn hard are our differences. As you get swept up in the busyness of the day, working through a difference of opinion with a colleague who drives you crazy is not high on your list of priorities. Making time to talk with the team about its purpose will need to wait another day because you are under a pressing deadline. Taking time with your team to talk about the weekend is mixing pleasure with business. "If everyone just did their work, we'd get more done."

Here is where the disregarded soft things become hard barriers to overcome. Slowly, the nature of relationships become perfunctory. Team cohesion erodes. In its place a climate takes root that feels caustic, toxic, impersonal, or just flat-out dull. Reinforcing our differences is our human drive to be surrounded by and befriend people who are like ourselves.

We become fascinated by those who fascinate in the same way we do.

To illustrate the science behind our innate ability to develop friendships with those like ourselves, let's look at a 2018 study from psychologists at UCLA and the Tuck School of Business, Dartmouth College. Researchers Carolyn Parkinson, Adam M. Kleinbaum, and Thalia Wheatley invited 279 MBA graduate students to take an online survey. The survey's purpose was identifying the social distances between friends. Think of the game Six Degrees of Kevin Bacon. The survey intended to identify which students had one degree of separation between them, or two, or three. For one degree of separation, the dyad—or pair—were marked as friends. More degrees of separation made friends become a friend of a friend, or a friend of a friend of a friend.

Here is where the study gets really interesting. A subset of the study participants had an MRI brain scan. While lying in the scanner, the students were shown a diverse mix of videos across different genres of film. The clips were selected because they tapped into a variety of emotions. The researchers wanted the participants engaged in the video content, not tuning out boring videos. Responses to the videos were then mapped to eighty distinct regions of the brain and correlated to the pairs of friends. The researchers wanted to see if those who were linked as friends had similar neural responses to the videos.

Here is where neural synchrony becomes important. After controlling for differences such as gender, ethnicity, nationality, and age, the researchers found that the students who were linked as friends shared similar neural responses. These similarities were linked to regions of the brain associated with: perspective-taking; what captures our attention; beliefs and expectations; goals and values; and general intelligence, knowledge, and abilities—or what psychologists call affective processing.[3]

So, what does this tell us? In short, people in our immediate circle of friends, including those at work, are more likely to interpret their environment similarly to us. Friends are more likely to share similar perspectives about issues in the workplace, for example. They also share similar beliefs about the role work plays in their lives and share similar values about life or other matters important to them. Going a bit deeper, Dr. Matthew Lieberman, a colleague of Parkinson and her team, observed that, "[Our] unique personal way of seeing the world is so central to who we are, that those who show signs of being our phenomenological comrades would be highly valued by us." *Phenomenological* refers to your belief system that guides how you think and make sense of your experiences. It's also associated with self-awareness.[4]

The study surfaces a powerful insight for leaders at all levels. Self-awareness, in all its awkwardness, is the best antidote to the destructive intolerance of differences. Leaders who build teams that think and act like them sacrifice the benefits of feeling valued, wanted, and welcomed.

Our brains evolved over many millennia to notice and respond to likenesses we share with others. It was a matter of life and death for our early ancestors. Today, our search for likeness is less about physical survival. It is our brain's way of helping us develop meaningful friendships that enrich our lives and well-being. The brain does not discriminate between friends in or outside of work. The truth is that shared neural responses are not the issue; it is our unchecked biases and resulting behaviors that skew the value of neural synchrony. A team composed of people that are too similar will develop blind spots to problems; the need to hear divergent ideas is ignored and differences in opinions and ideas are quickly dismissed. In the end, employees who do not want to play the game to fit in become outsiders, unwitting members of a club that they did not ask to join. The smart ones leave to find a place where their talents, contributions, and differences are sought out, valued, wanted, and welcomed.

FROM THE OUTSIDE LOOKING IN

It is a cool fall day. The sun is due west, signaling the pending transition to evening. In the autumn shade, lined up in a school courtyard, is an exuberant group of adolescent boys. As several of their classmates march in front of them, the young men begin to clap in unison. In response, the marching boys fall into a cadence matching the clapping rhythm. This is a scene from *Dead Poets Society*, the 1989 movie starring Robin Williams, Ethan Hawke, Robert Sean Leonard, and many other notable actors and actresses. Williams's character, John Keating, is a maverick English teacher with a keen ability to make classic literature and self-awareness a potent aphrodisiac.

As the boys become transfixed by the unison of their clapping and marching, John Keating joins in and then abruptly halts the fun. Quickly moving from fun to instructive, the endearing English teacher surfaces his point to the experiential exercise: Your originality is in jeopardy when conformity is the norm. Sure, your need, my need, our need for acceptance and belonging are undeniably central to the human experience of living. But the power of compliance as it spreads is mighty and can overwhelm our individuality.[5]

Consider the 2018 story involving former CEO and chairman of Papa John's, John Schnatter. In a *Forbes* article (that Schnatter refutes) journalist Noah Kirsch interviewed thirty-seven Papa John's employees—past and current—and recounted stories about the rampant bro culture in the fast-casual restaurant chain. What helped the toxic behavior flourish? Conformity. Executives and board members shared stories with Kirsch of alleged misconduct including spying on employees, racist remarks, and misogynistic actions. Schnatter's loyalists benefited from their silence. But it was Schnatter's own racist remarks that were his undoing.[6] As I write about the Papa John's culture crisis, it is not known what fate awaits Schnatter.

Schnatter's alleged actions serve as an example of how company culture suffers under conformity. The bro culture reveals a dangerous, narrow-mindedness stemming from outdated traditions of success and power. The consequences have been dire. When leaders fail to update their antiquated guidance systems, they often lose their position in the company. Their legacy will not be one that history looks upon favorably.

The media loves to tell quick stories. Sometimes those stories entertain or inform, but too often their brevity leaves out the deeper parts. In this case, what about the fallout that employees and managers are left to navigate? Or the collective sigh of relief when the truth is finally out? How does a company move forward to rebuild its culture?

Belonging is a powerful preventative to the kind of behavior that sullies organizations and destroys reputations. That mini-list of travesties includes leaders feigning ignorance when reports of bullying or sexual harassment surface. The stain from these secrets allows incivility to become the norm. What's more, the deniability is a selfish act; it's the leaders' Hail Mary, attempting to avoid responsibility for destroying lives and the deterioration of a company's purpose and financial success.

It is naive to believe that belonging is a cure-all tonic to what ails toxic workplaces. In such workplaces, belonging becomes a place to start, a shift away from alienation. The belonging practices provide an intentional path forward to help create team cohesion and make good use of our innate human desires to be part of something bigger than ourselves.

CONTAGIOUS CONFORMITY AND DISORDER ASCENDING

In Latin *concordia salus* is translated as "well-being through harmony." Apply the phrase to our conversation about belonging and a new insight emerges. A company's cultural health contributes to its effectiveness. An unwell or toxic workplace depletes people and resources. Business results are capped as if hitting a ceiling. Human potential is diminished. If the environment is not healthy, neither is the well-being of those working in it. Employee behaviors that contribute to toxicity keep harmony off-kilter and unattainable. Sure, pockets of excellence may exist, but it costs the leader and employees a great degree of dis-ease.

Schnatter's behaviors went unchecked for years, and he wasted time and energy to keep people quiet. Similarly, the shoemaker Nike is recovering from forcing out nine executives, who were creating a hostile work environment for women. In response to a *New York Times* investigation, Nike explained that the harassers were a small-but-coordinated group of managers. Alleged actions ranged from vulgar language, degrading name-calling, discussions of women's breasts in emails, and even a manager bragging about carrying condoms. Unfortunately, the investigation also uncovered an inhuman, fear-based response from HR. The claims appeared to not be taken seriously. Others were admonished for not dealing with the situation personally before coming to HR.[7] This pattern of response is much like that of universities, the US women's gymnastics leadership team, and even companies like Uber. Reportedly, the Nike executives accused of harassment protected one another and looked the other way when told about incidents.[8] Employee behaviors are contagious—positive or negative.

In order to thrive, organizations need to understand how to maximize our differences to maximize collaborative effort for the betterment of the company. This is challenging yet very important. Anyone who turns away from claims or evidence of actions that prevent people from feeling valued, wanted, and welcomed, contribute to toxic contagions. People are not cogs.

Your colleagues have life experiences invaluable to solving wicked problems. Learn their stories. You will discover what's underneath reveals the connection points that build unstoppable work tribes.

TOXIC INSTABILITY

I want to bring you back to the phenomenon of neural synchrony. While it is mostly viewed as a positive neurological occurrence associated with friendships, there are interferences that undermine its benefits. Those interferences are injurious behaviors that poison team cohesion.

While entire books have been written about the ill-effects of bad apples at work, I want to limit the discussion here to three toxic behaviors. For the purposes of belonging, we will look at the toxic behaviors of bullying, rejection, and ostracism.

An interesting study out of Harvard Business School uncovered these unnerving findings:

- One in twenty workers are terminated for toxic behavior.
- If the toxic employee is not terminated after the first year, their chances of being fired are about equal to an average worker's performance.
- Toxic workers tend to be more productive, but their work quality is low.
- In the long run, toxic employees do not contribute to measurable business outcomes.

- The work environment is the biggest influence on toxic behaviors.
- A conservative estimate to replace employees who left because of a toxic colleague is $12,849. This does not include potential litigation, lost business, damaged reputation, training costs, turnover costs, and costs associated with low employee morale.
- The definition of a toxic employee is someone who engages in behavior that is harmful to the company and its employees.[9]

Also fascinating is the finding that toxic employees claim to be rule followers. They present themselves as overly confident in their talents and hold themselves in high regard. The researchers posit that this employee type eludes quick termination because of their productivity, an unfortunate blow to team morale and individual satisfaction with work. It is yet another example of bad actors who, by slow management response, are permitted to lower the performance bar.[10]

TOXIC BEHAVIOR ONE: BULLYING

Take a look at the short list of statements shown in Table 4.1, but keep in mind that it is a partial list. Next to each statement mark the frequency of your experience at your workplace, keeping a six-month time frame in mind.

TABLE 4.I: BULLYING QUESTIONNAIRE

Item	Never	Now & Then	Monthly	Weekly
Someone withholding information that affects your performance				
Having your opinions ignored				
Hints or signals from others that you should quit your job				
Repeated reminders of your errors and mistakes				
Having false allegations made against you				
Being shouted at or being the target of spontaneous anger				

The questions are part of the globally accepted research tool, Negative Acts Questionnaire. One of its more intriguing design elements is that the word *bully* is never used. Instead, the Norwegian professors who created the questionnaire separated bullying behaviors into three categories: work-related bullying (items one and two), person-related bullying (items three and four), and physically intimidating bullying (items five and six).[11]

You may have noticed that some of the statements could be interpreted in several ways. Some employees may not view having their opinions ignored as bullying. This, in part, is what makes bullying hard to address as a manager or even for HR. While it may be debatable which behaviors reflect bullying and which are "just part of business," research shows that workers view these behaviors as negative. What makes bullying a pernicious problem is that it is a one-two punch of (one) negative interactions that are (two) persistent.

Bullies do not always act covertly. Overt bullying begins to spread the negativity to those who witness or hear about the behavior. Letting a bully continue his or her reign of terror will not only compromise the health of the team but also destroy employees' well-being. The contagion spreads to employees' homes too.[12]

Belonging may not survive bullying. You can help prevent bullying or teach employees skills to mitigate its destruction. To teach employees how to prevent being pulled into a bully's gravitational pull, tap into the influential benefits of autonomy and self-efficacy.

Neutralize the Bully's Influence with Autonomy

Adults prefer to apply their experiences, strengths, and talents to problem solving. We do not like being told how to do something unless we ask for input or guidance. When you give employees the resources to effectively work, research finds that this helps them cope with the demands, including working alongside a bully. This is called job demands-resources model. In simple terms, the positives outweigh the negatives. When you provide employees with growth opportunities and the necessary tools to be successful, and when you help them achieve their goals, the negative impact of a bully strengthens targets' resolve to ignore that bully.[13] I suggest this possible solution with one major caveat: actively work to remove the perpetrator from your team and the organization.

Build Employees' Confidence and Self-Awareness

Self-efficacy is our belief that we have the abilities and strength to overcome challenges that may interfere with our success. The awareness that comes with self-efficacy is a lifetime pursuit. Organizations can support employees' exploration of their strengths and apply them on how to solve problems. Employees who are confident in their abilities and strengths see working with a bully (or any difficult task or situation) as a problem to solve. For some, the approach may be to ignore the bully or stand up for themselves. Low self-efficacy is associated with viewing difficult tasks or situations as threats. Unfortunately, employees who have not invested time to raise their own self-awareness may be trapped by focusing on their own negative emotional reactions to the bully.

In part 3 I explore solutions for inspiring a sense of belonging. Right now I will say this: invest time or money in helping employees learn about themselves. Our research shows that companies and teams with a high sense of belonging prioritize workshops, self-assessments, on-the-job assignments, and coaching or mentoring. Think of self-awareness as a verb;

if you don't actively "do it," you or your employees will stagnate and risk flaming out under high-pressure expectations. Self-efficacy is not only invaluable to dulling the influence of a bully, but it also helps promote both team cohesion and effectively addressing conflict.

TOXIC BEHAVIOR TWO: OSTRACISM

As if it were an early version of the TV show *Survivor*, men in ancient Greece who were viewed as having too much power were voted out of their city. The ostracized man had to depart Greece for a decade, leaving behind his family and possessions and cut off from contacting them. It's not as if the castaway had a smartphone to text his loved ones, tweet his philosophical musings, or make a quick video call. Ostracism meant you were off the island, and there was no way back to see family and friends. Today, however, ostracism is arguably and sadly even more cruel.

Throughout our evolution, our brains developed a finely honed detection system, which helps us interpret signals when we are not wanted, valued, or welcomed. Cognitively and emotionally speaking, warning bells alert you that something is not right.[14] Call it an instinct or gut feeling; we all have walked into a room and immediately sensed that we should not be there. Imagine, then, observing that your presence is repeatedly ignored. Research from 2015 found that when we feel ignored, the psychological damage is worse than if we were being bullied or rejected by a person or team.[15] We are wired to belong. We have learned to develop connections and relationships to get along in life and work. To be socially ignored cuts deep into our experience of living. Ostracized Greek men could at least interact with citizens in their new city.

To learn how we experience ostracism, scientists created Cyberball, an online computer simulation. If you were a participant in the study, you would be partnered to play a virtual game of catch with two other online players. After a few rounds of passing the ball among all three players, the others stop throwing the ball to you. In fact, they never throw the ball to you again. No matter what you did, they would not pass you the ball. Suddenly the simulation ends. How would you feel?

Those study participants did not like being excluded. One scenario placed players inside an fMRI (functional magnetic resonance imaging) machine. With their brain activity measured, the study found that players who were ostracized showed different brain activity than the other players. The ignored players consistently showed brain activity in their dorsal anterior cingulate cortex and the anterior insula. These are the same areas of your brain that respond to physical pain like breaking your leg.[16]

There are many variations on how Cyberball is used to understand the impact of ostracism. The creator of the game, Kipling Williams, traces the studies that use his online game. Studies consistently find that ostracism hurts. Chronic social exclusion can lead people to give up finding reasons to belong. No doubt about it: this is a severe and serious outcome.

"It's just business" is not a repellent for feeling isolated. Any leader who believes belonging needs to be part of the experience of work must overtly communicate and model that working together is how stunning results are achieved.

TOXIC BEHAVIOR THREE: REJECTION

If you have not witnessed or experienced workplace rejection, you may have a hard time imagining a scenario where it is inappropriate. The reality is that we all experience not getting something we deeply want sometime in our careers—maybe a promotion or being asked to lead an important project, for example. This type of rejection is part of life. Toxic rejection, however, could be compared to how many feel when picked last for a game of kickball: intentionally overlooked because neither team captain wants you on his team. At work, that type of rejection is an overt gesture that clearly signals that you are not wanted.

What type of rejection can be toxic to a culture of belonging? Receiving cruel feedback on the quality of your work that is personal, perhaps even unwarranted, and does not help you improve, is an expression of rejection. Another form that could thwart belonging is the blatant denial of a request to participate in an activity, giving no response except "No."

When we are rejected we experience pain like that associated with being ostracized. The damage, however, tends to be easier for our social natures to deal with and overcome. Researchers consistently find that our brain's wiring for belonging will push us to retaliate against those who reject us. The difference, however, is this form of social exclusion impels us to seek relationships where we do experience feeling valued, wanted, and welcomed. When I was a kid, I had a clown punching bag. Whenever I'd punch it, the clown bounced back up. That is how we tend to respond to rejection: we get knocked down but get back up and move on.

But here is a word of caution to help a culture of belonging to thrive. Teammates or people leaders who make rejection personal and malicious can trigger dysfunctional behavior in others. Not everyone will simply bounce back and carry on. In some studies those who were denied feeling valued, wanted, and welcomed learned to be quiet and not draw attention to themselves. For example, one study revealed that subjects excluded from a group silently drank orange juice made with vinegar. They did not spit it out or complain about the taste. Resignation is a terrible conclusion. Excluded subjects in studies also ate more unhealthy foods, gave up more quickly on difficult tasks, and even struggled to pay attention.[17] A learned response to being rejected? Absolutely. Rejection leads to aggressive behavior toward those cruel enough to dish it out. In every model company we studied for this book, there was no tolerance for cruelty. Feedback that does not maintain a person's dignity or that is not shared with respect is malicious. In high-performing teams, feedback is constructive and includes discussion about how to improve.

The silver lining around rejection is that it can be overcome. Perhaps the pain does not cut as deep as being ignored or bullied. The need for friendships, no matter the place or our role, mediates the psychological pain associated with antisocial behavior. In one Cyberball study, when a new player was introduced, the excluded participant shifted attention to the "new guy" to gain acceptance from him.[18] Additionally, studies show that helping excluded people become more self-aware reduces their aggressive and selfish behaviors.

What does this mean for leading a team or a company's culture?

The insidious indifference, which too often leads to inaction because of the prevailing belief that nothing will change, is unfortunate, at a minimum. Worse, the workforce is trained to look out for their own safety and keep their heads down. The consequences are destructive and radically alter the ability to deliver productive results. The focus is not on wowing customers or exceeding expectations. Instead, employees, including people leaders, waste their energy avoiding or retaliating against politics and injustices. And the sad part of this toxic instability? The longer it is allowed to fester, the more the sewage, if you will, becomes accepted as the norm.

A shared culture of belonging is hard to create, particularly when behaviors that damage relationships are tolerated. Perhaps we did not know in the twentieth century that queen bees and jerks were bad for business? I believe that we have known all along. Within all of us is the knowledge that we need one another to live, thrive, have fun, and make a difference. It's innate; it's in our brain's wiring. It's also in our individual memories linked to events when we were not valued, wanted, or welcomed.

From the moment our ancestors learned how to create fire, to the first samurai settlement in California, to today's unsettling world, humanity's story consistently reinforces that achievement is possible when we collaborate. If you recall Doug Conant from part 1, this former CEO of Campbell's had a moment of reckoning with his leadership team. To turn around the ailing company, Conant said this to the leaders:

> Enough is enough. I hope all of you want to be part of this company going forward, but you have to lead in a way that's going to build the world's most extraordinary food company. If you don't want to sign up for that, you shouldn't be here.[19]

Extraordinary emerges only when people focus together on what's possible.

Toxic behaviors expunge the extraordinary. In its place is a vague notion of lost potential that evaporates over time.

CHAPTER 5

OF THE WAYS OF MISFITS, MAVERICKS, AND RENEGADES

Grass Also Grows in Cracks of Concrete

The world is a very puzzling place. If you're not willing to be puzzled, you just become a replica of someone else's mind.

—Noam Chomsky

Work is like Henry Ford's first Model T. Before the Model T rolled off the factory assembly line, consumers could not afford to replace their horses with a car. Without knowing it was possible to mass produce a car, customers stuck with what they knew—the horse and buggy. Similarly, a large number of executives, leaders, and employees do not know that their awareness of how we should work is ill-suited for today's realities.

However, like Henry Ford, you may see a pattern that many overlook or are simply too busy to notice. You, the workplace maverick, may see the inefficiencies in the way we work together. (If you didn't, you would not have bought this book.) Many of today's employees are overwhelmed by work and underwhelmed by its value in their lives. Dystopian workplaces—dreary, gray, and uneventful—have become too real, too common.

The pattern that you see (or will see in a moment) is your next, or perhaps first, rebellious leadership act. Like Ford, you see that our lives are more complicated. A horse was no longer prudent in the twentieth century for bustling life in the city. People needed a solution to mirror their reality. In the twenty-first century, we are pulled in many directions, manage competing priorities, deal with polarities that boggle the mind, and in between taking the kids to practice and caring for our aging parents, we schedule date nights and sex to "stay in touch." Notice I did not mention work. In short, how we work today is out of step with how we live. In the absence of knowing what to change, or that change is even needed, the lull from the status quo medicates our minds. But, as I've hinted several times already, you see the pattern that can disrupt and help unify work with life.

OF THE WAYS OF TODAY'S BUSINESS REBELS

Henry Ford, an early business rebel, observed that, "If you wait for the customer to tell you what to do, you're too late. My customers didn't want a Model T, they wanted a faster horse."

The logic upon which Ford makes his observation reveals an interesting pattern. Think of it as containing four stages from which rebels—misfits, mavericks, and renegades—can pluck out a compelling idea that ultimately matters to their beneficiaries. This pattern is also useful when applied to innovating work with belonging.

FIGURE 5.1: REBEL'S PATTERN FOR CHANGE

Rebel's Pattern for Change

Unaware
There is little to no awareness of the need to change

Status Quo
Because unawareness is low or absent, people are fine with how things are

Rebellious Action
A person comes along and observes that change is needed, but the solution is not obvious to most

New Understanding
Through transformative actions (simple to complex) a need for change is understood and a new way helps to resolve the once hidden problem

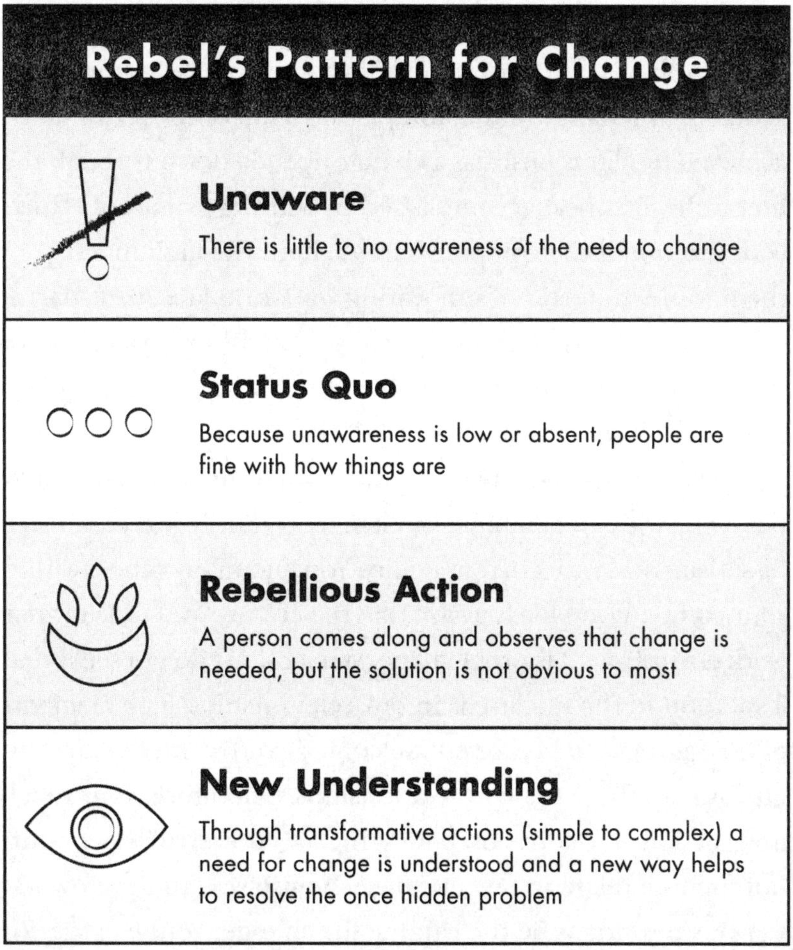

As discoveries that shape our understanding occur faster than we can cognitively process, most of us do not recognize the change opportunity. Much like Ford's Model T, Steve Jobs's iPhone also fits the rebel's pattern for change. We had no idea we could find greater efficiencies in many—but not all—areas of living by walking around talking on a device that also helps us work. Not all change needs are imperceptible. But those who learn to see the pattern can impact lives, including employees' and coworkers' lives.

Figure 5.1 shows a simplified explanation of the pattern that leads to important innovations, even workplace innovations. Whole-scale change of the workplace is a tall order. It cannot be achieved by CEOs pushing a change agenda down through the hierarchy. It is best accomplished by uniting grassroot efforts with the top of the company's food chain through meeting in the middle. In terms of innovating the workplace, your part is to lead the charge for your team, so you all experience work that is both meaningful and fulfilling. The panacea we are pursuing is *belonging at work*.

The rebel's pattern begins with an awareness. It may or may not come with an epiphany, but it most certainly surfaces with a dissatisfaction with current reality. You and many others within your company are likely aware that the culture and tone of your work environment is problematic. What others do not see is that a solution to the malaise is in our relationships. The elements of belonging—to be valued, welcomed, and wanted—tap into our human drive to be in relationships. Therefore, your rebellious action is to focus on belonging as a powerful way to shift how people relate to one another, themselves, and their work. Let this new focus be the catalyst for change. You, *à la manière de* Ford and Jobs, are raising a new awareness. Yours may not be as capitalistic as a car or new technology, but it is learning and showing and learning more how our need for one another helps drive powerful business results.

ARISTOTLE AND THE MEAN

When Aristotle examined the nature of virtues—the feelings and actions that shape our daily living—he warned against "excess and . . . deficiency." Aristotle argued that virtues mediate the extremes and position a person "to be in a good state and to perform their functions well."[1] In layman's terms, Aristotle is advocating for finding the center point, the mean, that supports your efforts to do well in your relationships, society, and work. Similarly, when inspiring a sense of belonging in your teams, be mindful of the "excess and deficiency." These extremes represent the contrast between taking things too far and not taking enough action—inspiring cliques that create chaos versus lone wolves who long for connection.

It is possible to have too much belongingness. The same is true for the absence of it. And when belonging no longer shapes relationships and workplace environments, it is replaced by any number of alternatives that, frankly, are far easier to maintain. In place of belonging can be loneliness, rejection, fitting in, or other mindsets and behaviors that continually reinforce a workplace feudal system.

Aristotle warned against veering away from the mean. Today sociologists and psychologists remind us that while we want to belong, we also want to be distinct. These two extremes are seemingly contradictory, but in reality the human need for distinctiveness and familiarity is central to how we work in teams and groups.

Professor Marilyn Brewer of Northwestern University, Chicago, explains the above polarities in her optimal distinctiveness model. The essence of her model applied to belonging is this: Each of us can experience feeling valued, wanted, and welcomed when our needs for both individuation and being part of a team are equal. When teams learn to embrace the human need to be similar and unique—in equal parts and at the same time—they create the conditions for loyalty.[2] There is room for nonconformists, conservatives, and any other personality types.

When too much of a good thing like belonging continues unchecked, it will undermine performance. As Aristotle warned, our well-being can become compromised. From there, the unraveling of team and individual identity thrusts upon people a dynamic not useful to anyone. Who watches the balance between the distinct and the same?

You. It takes a bit of a misfit heart to believe that a leader's role now includes intentionally crafting methods to hold teams together.

Is this a fair expectation for leaders?

I'll say this: part of a leader's role is to inspire, motivate, and help release human potential. Any disinterest in the aforementioned minimum requirements makes a manager ill-suited for this role. This expectation is fair because it requires something that you and I and anyone else reading this book understand. Indeed, you are a familiar topic to yourself.

THE WAKE YOU MAKE

"So, someone who's very mindful of their wake and has the mature and sobering understanding of how powerful [his or her] wake is . . . is the kind of person we want to be connected to,"[3] explains Kip Tindell, cofounder, chairman, and former CEO for The Container Store. Today The Container Store is a publicly traded company. In 2017, this mecca for organizational diehards (I resemble that remark) had net sales of $787.4 million.[4] It has been listed as a top place to work for nineteen years. No company achieves such sustained levels of success without investing in its leaders and employees. Included in that investment is helping leaders understand what Tindell calls their *wake*.

Wake is a boating term. It is the trail of water swelling into waves behind a moving boat. The faster the boat, the bigger the waves from its wake. Similarly, your actions have a cause and effect. The awareness of that effect is what Tindell believes is central to a great people leader. But as he would tell you, awareness is not nearly enough.

The way you show up impacts the stickiness and experience of belonging. Your effectiveness, long term and short term, are directly linked to the quality of the relationships you have with your team and colleagues. Strongly influencing the tone of your relationships is how you relate with others. Using the company hierarchy to determine your relationships with employees is "inefficient and undermines the long-term viability of a company," Tindell says in his measured Texas drawl.

Today's workers are ambitious. Younger leaders are accused of being impatient, though this is a bit hypocritical. Most of us are impatient in our youth. And some elder leaders never picked up a lesson on patience throughout life. Whining over the lack of loyalty from today's employees is a disguised longing for "how things used to be." It used to be that the higher up the corporate food chain a manager went, the more deference and respect employees had for him or her. The automatic loyalty and respect are not gone; the context is different. The most effective and relatable leaders are the ones who can maneuver within the hierarchy without relying on it to inspire employees' commitment. As for the leader's wake, the hierarchy is not a reason to justify behaviors that tear at the social fabric holding teams together. "Consumers are [voting] with their pocket books more and more. [They] are supporting businesses that are mindful of its wake," Tindell told me.[5] The same mindset influences how employees view their boss.

In terms of showing your team that they are valued, wanted, and welcomed, your wake with positive intent has a highly desirable effect. Tindell has witnessed the unifying effects of belonging: "[Employees] feel better about themselves and ideally part of something bigger than them. They also feel needed and important."[6] Consequently, a leader's wake that is created by an intentional focus on belonging replaces employees' insecurities with pride. You need these outcomes to achieve astonishing results.

You are the first domino. The chain reaction from your leadership is felt throughout your team. What move will you make? Will it be intentional? Concerning the ways of misfits, mavericks, and renegades, the effective ones share a common pursuit, an evolving sense of self-awareness.

MIRROR, MIRROR

Does a mirror simply reflect what is or does it reveal the truth? It's an ancient question, rich in musings from poets extolling the symbolic meaning of the mirror. Even Robert Steven Kaplan, the current president and CEO of Dallas's Federal Reserve Bank (and former professor at Harvard Business School), taps into the mirror's symbolism in exploring human potential in his book *What to Ask the Person in the Mirror.*[7]

The mirror can only show what is. The person looking into it gives meaning to what is seen. Truth is subjective and fraught with embellishments and understatements. As you peer at yourself in a mirror, you make meaning of the scar on your chin or the zit that no one really sees (but to you is a flashing neon sign buzzing, "Look at me!"). Amid the story-making, heavy sighs, and even smiles of contentment, looking at ourselves in the mirror reflects our discomfort with examining who we are, what we believe, and how the stories we tell ourselves project lies and truths on the form seen in the mirror. This is what makes self-awareness painful for many adults.

In workshops where I have leaders practice self-awareness through journaling, I inevitably hear complaints and audible sighs of annoyance. "I don't like spending time thinking about myself," complain executives, CEOs, and middle managers. Yet research consistently shows that spending time critically evaluating our thoughts and actions yields undeniably important benefits: better decisions, a calmer mind, more emerging leaders stepping into leadership roles, and even vulnerability.

Amanda, a popular server at Canlis Restaurant, observed how vulnerability is key to her team's success. "If you're wishy-washy and you don't necessarily know [to] what you want to belong, there's no way that you're going to be successful in actually belonging." She adds that it is essential to take time to examine what you believe is important. If you cannot care for yourself, then how can you lead effectively?[8]

Staring at yourself in the mirror takes a willingness to be vulnerable and to listen to the internal critics. Dr. Brené Brown places vulnerability at the heart of belonging. You may (hopefully) choose to invest your time and show your compassion in building an environment that evokes a sense of belonging. However, some of your team may not appreciate your actions, at least at first. At the same time some will see what you are attempting and champion your actions. Despite the possibility of rejection, you act anyway. This is what Brown calls vulnerability.[9]

Inclinations and Actions for Leading Outside the Mirror

Noam Chomsky's quote at the beginning of this chapter elucidates a belief important to mitigating belonging gone sideways. The inspiring and sometime-intoxicating nature of finding your tribe increases the chances of blind spots. Those blind spots can hinder observing dysfunctions that disregard nonconformity and incline toward fanaticism. By *fanaticism* I mean insisting on a loyalty to the team that has not been earned. Chomsky is not advocating that we remain puzzled by the world. He is advocating that we embrace the perplexing realities of life outside the symbolic mirror. Going one step further, he urges that good old-fashioned thinking is requisite to self-awareness.

As Bruce and I analyzed the interview data, self-awareness stories continually surfaced. These stories, predominately positive, centered on a range of work-life realities: success, job satisfaction, intrinsic motivation, vulnerability, team unity, supporting others, sticking up for colleagues, and overcoming conflict. Interestingly, self-awareness was commonly linked to employees' bosses modeling it.

This points to a curious pairing of inclinations and actions; we can most effectively challenge the status quo by remaining intrigued in how we make sense of and affect our environment. It is irresponsible to be a misfit and remain clueless of the implications: people and results create an endless loop of cause and effect. Your actions are contagious. Be mindful of what you spread.

Let's examine a central influence to applying your version of renegade and remaining aware of what you spread. If you have ever worked with a coach, you likely heard the phrase "how you show up." For the more logically inclined, this phrase can be off-putting. If, however, you put it in the context of getting along and getting ahead, how you show up is really about your presence.

Simply observe what happens when you enter a room. Or watch for how people defer to you—or don't. What is the tone in your relationships? To help ease the influence of the superiority bias (a social bias that downplays our undesirable qualities and overestimates our desirable ones in comparison to other people) and help you make sense of your presence and impact as objectively as possible, I want to introduce you to two personality categories: adaptors and maintainers.[10]

Adaptors and maintainers are personality types that psychologists have continually validated and deepened our understanding of for more than four decades. They are linked to a social behavior called impression management. While the term impression management may sound manipulative, like a personal branding strategy used by politicians, it is something we all engage in to get along and get ahead. Impression management is a set of nuanced social behaviors used to influence how others evaluate us and to gain their approval.[11] Like belonging, it is something we developed to survive. It helps us work collaboratively and cooperatively.

You will identify with one of the personality types more than the other, so let's take a look at how adaptors and maintainers are different. But first, here are the three characteristics common to both types.

1. Desiring to be socially appropriate
2. Reading social cues
3. Controlling one's behavior in response to social cues[12]

The differences between adaptors and maintainers are in their *responses* to these three common characteristics. Adaptors are chameleon-like and motivated by having a positive, favorable image within teams or groups. Maintainers remain true to themselves no matter the context and are motivated by reinforcing beliefs that uphold what they believe about themselves.

It may be tempting to say adaptors are wishy-washy or fake, acting in any manner that makes them likable, and that maintainers are brave to uphold their values and be true to their sense of identity. These quick conclusions, however, would be misleading.

Compare the three characteristics listed above to the adaptor and maintainer definitions. Different insights begin to emerge. Adapters are more adept at monitoring their behavior to fit the circumstances. For example, they understand that some work situations require gracefully surfacing a contrary viewpoint, such as when meeting with a colleague known to get emotional when challenged. Maintainers, on the other hand, will act in a manner true to how they see themselves: as confident people.

Once, when working with an underperforming team, I designed a meeting for them to develop agreements on how they would talk and treat one another. One of the outspoken teammates said, "What you see is what you get. If you are doing something that betrays trust, I will call you out on it. After all, you want to know the truth." This is a maintainer position. This teammate was unwilling to consider adjusting based on the context and the person. It was more important that she "be who she is" than that she communicate to maximize team performance.

Which personality type best contributes to high performance? Researchers since the early 1970s continually find that adapters are more effective at acquiring status, power, and control of resources at work. They also are viewed more favorably in establishing meaningful relationships. The impression adapters give to others positions them to reach manager and senior manager roles. It is important, however, to note that maintainers do care about how others view them. The difference is that their impression must align with their true self. Table 5.2 shows a breakdown of the primary differences between these two personality types.

TABLE 5.2: ADAPTERS AND MAINTAINERS [13]

Adapters	Maintainers
Gains favor by intentional actions	Attempts to please for personal gain
Viewed as competent when sharing about their talents, unique skills, abilities, and qualifications	Viewed as conceited when sharing about their talents, unique skills, abilities, and qualifications
Seen as dedicated in their work	Believed to maintain an air of superiority over others
Viewed as likeable, competent, and dedicated	Viewed as intimidating and bossy

It may be tempting to pigeonhole adapters as phonies. When researchers studied this possibility, they found that adapters' chameleon-like abilities cause them anxiety and stress because of their constant adaptations to social situations. As a result, the anxiety and stress can undermine the positive image they built. Adapters also report lower company commitment. Some research findings revealed that adapters experience weaker social ties with colleagues.

Adapters need to define their leadership philosophy (personal core values and purpose) and establish a practice of self-care. Maintainers should also establish a practice of self-care, because learning to flex in different social settings will contribute to growth and stretch them outside comfort zones.

Be Consistent and Knowable

The barriers to belonging are as daunting or scalable as you make them to be. On your side is human nature, our inclination for camaraderie. Human nature is a puzzle that confounds and, at the same time, inspires. How you make sense of it and learn from it depends on your willingness to examine your beliefs, biases, and their impact on business and people.

Whether your traits align with those of adapters or maintainers, *watch your wake.* I tell my clients to be consistent and knowable. Be consistent in your core leadership practices. When there is predictability in your leader actions, you create ease and familiarity. These two outcomes are important counterpoints to our overwhelmed, maxed-out, tech-driven work environments. When employees can anticipate your response to crises or know your hot buttons and passions, that knowledge helps your team work together. You set the tone. Research from Gallup and the Hay Group came to the same conclusion regarding a leader's impact on employees' experience of work: a leader's style accounts for 70 percent of that experience.[14]

Since this part of the book focuses on the hard parts of creating a sense of belonging, we need to examine the influence and impact of dysfunctional, or skunked, managers.

Skunked Management

What is skunked management?

The failure to create enduring, shared, meaningful results by demonstrating behaviors that negate progress and impact people, teams, the company, and—ultimately—customers.

An estimated 13 to 36 percent of Americans have dysfunctional managers. Using 2018 full-time employment numbers from the US government (129.98 million employees), approximately 17 to 46 million Americans endure management who negatively influence employee health and quality of life while preventing belonging from emerging.[15]

A slow-burn discussion among leadership theorists, consultants, and academics calls for basic mental-health training for managers. The intent is not to train managers to become psychologists or therapists. After all, it is a business environment. Managers who act as therapists would likely confuse performance levels with "that's just who they are," and they are not in a position to diagnose employees' mental health. Instead, by training managers to (1) better understand how their behavior influences others, (2) recognize signs of burnout or distress, and (3) have conversations associated with motivation, we can better tackle long-standing performance issues.

Consider these horrendous numbers that have continually surfaced for at least two decades. Gallup's research finds that more than 80 percent of managers do not have the requisite skills to be a leader. In a study of more than seven thousand employees, half said that they left a company to get away from a skunked manager.[16] These numbers, however damaging and convicting of management malpractice, may not be persuasive enough for CEOs to invest in training managers on the effects of underwhelming leadership. Factor in how woefully inadequate some managers' skills are to motivate their employees or effectively adjust to shifting priorities and executives might see the ill-effects of those absent table-stakes leadership qualities. In 2017, Gallup uncovered that less than 25 percent of managers knew how to motivate employees and only 12 percent knew how to set work priorities.[17] The stench from the century-old belief that managers know best still lingers in business offices across the country.

It is seductive to hold on to the outmoded belief that managers, sitting atop the pyramid, do not need to change how they show up and lead. It's not only seductive but also convenient. When the world changes around us and we deny such shifts occur, societies fail to thrive. The same is true for companies and their workers. The equation is, frankly, quite simple: Arrogance + Ignorance − Acknowledgment of Fear ≠ Change.

Literature on dysfunctional leaders holds basic agreement that poor management, its related behaviors, and their effects fall on a continuum. For our purposes, I need to narrow the scope to the effects of dysfunction on a sense of belonging.

A SILENT, INCONVENIENT CRISIS

Why are many organizations slow to strategize how to overcome damage inflicted by poorly developed leadership? First, they need willingness at the top to financially invest in the solutions and requisite professional talent that can speed up this skill shift. I believe a second reason is linked to the difficulty of behavior change. Upskilling leaders who had a traditional business upbringing requires their willingness to unlearn practices that damage growth and psychological well-being: control, abuse of positional and resource powers, and weak appreciation for diversity, for example.

The continuum of dysfunctional management behaviors ranges from some impact to serious impact on employees and results. Researchers from the University of Louisville in Kentucky studied the effects of dysfunction and placed them on a continuum from low to high severity.

On the low end are effects such as lower employee satisfaction and organizational commitment. Turnover increases and productivity decreases as the dysfunctional behaviors worsen. Self-esteem lowers as emotional exhaustion and psychological distress increase. The more severe the behavior—or the longer the dysfunctional manager sticks around—the more people begin mimicking those behaviors. The penultimate damage is on employees' families, marriages, relationships, and on their physical, emotional, and mental health.[18]

The shortened string of above examples reveals significant barriers to experiencing a sense of belonging. The negative effects from the actions of managers with low self-awareness, or who remain "stuck" as maintainers, or who are simply unwilling to grow range from high to low impacts.

The researchers from University of Louisville placed dysfunctional behaviors in a two-by-two grid. The behaviors ranged from annoyances to causing trauma and have low-to-high impacts on direct reports and even colleagues. Their research is worth reviewing for a full list of the behaviors.[19] For our purposes, it is important to know that every behavior mapped out can contribute to loneliness or alienation. Here is a sample of the behaviors:

- Taking undue credit for other people's work
- Withholding information
- Overworking employees
- Holding favors hostage
- Giving someone the silent treatment
- Reminding employees of their weaknesses
- Explosive outbursts and yelling
- Public scorn and denigration

The behaviors above undermine or decimate the experience of feeling valued, wanted, and welcomed. Misfits, mavericks, and renegades are not the subversive types. Instead, they are the artisans who craft compelling environments that inspire high performance. A defining belief of these leader-artisans is that they are responsible for unleashing human potential. The priority of this belief, and the time spent crafting belonging-inspired climates, is tantamount to operational and strategic responsibilities.

Without exception, every company included in our study had owners, CEOs, executives, and employees who shared stories of ongoing discussions about expectations. Grounding those conversations were constant references to the team's or company's purpose. The frequency of these two topics—expectations and purpose—supported a shared belief that the team's success is more important than any brilliant superstar performance or steady-eddies contributions. There was simply no tolerance for a phoning-in performance. High performance is like a garden;

ignored, it becomes overwhelmed with weeds and overgrowth, lacking a coherent design. Daily and weekly care of a garden highlights its natural and manicured beauty. High-performing teams require leaders who understand the importance of remaining focused not just on goals but, more importantly, on how the team achieves goals. Daily and weekly maintenance is required. No team will flourish when its people leader, assuming there is one, ignores or delays required maintenance.

Dysfunction is a function of neglect. Leader negligence will choke belonging. Whether in too much belonging, from dysfunctional practices that reinforce fitting in and conformity, or in the absence of belonging, from thoughtlessness and arrogance, team entropy will be the victor. In the end, it is the self-aware leader's diligence to observe and respond that can usurp entropy.

WHERE GRASS ALSO GROWS

"I like it when a flower or a little tuft of grass grows through a crack in the concrete; It's so f%$in' heroic," observed the late George Carlin. The comedian's observation about nature reveals the audacity of defying what is. How is it possible that a patch of grass, or a flower, or even a tree can sprout and grow from the side of a rock? It is not *why* or *how* it happens that matters, but that it *does* happen. Likewise, your contributions as a leader to inspire heroics, encourage the audacious, and defy the traditional in supporting your team's need to thrive are just as beautiful. Call me a romantic or an idealist. Though

OF THE WAYS OF MISFITS, MAVERICKS, AND RENEGADES

if you were to witness what we saw at Canlis, The Container Store, LinkedIn, or Barry-Wehmiller, you too would appreciate what happens when a team does not have to worry about the ill effects of weak relationships. The impact on the company and its employees' lives is nothing short of humanity showing its best side.

It matters if you identify as an adapter or a maintainer, a misfit, maverick, or renegade. What matters most, however, is how you invite belonging to be part of your team's experience of work. Playing it safe or defying the rules are simply stylistic ways that you can lead your team to astonishing results.

As Kip Tindell asserts, you need to observe your wake. This awareness is the opening to seeing how you influence those around you. Like the grass that finds its roots in the cracks of cement, you can show your version of heroics. Influencing a sense of belonging is a powerful way to unite your tribe—a valiant act.

One version of a cliché asserts that there can be too much of a good thing. Mae West's version delightfully spins the quote to embrace how wonderful too much of a good thing can be. What matters most is your take on it. Perhaps the dismal, dreary grind of work can use a heavy-handed dose of belonging. Or perhaps your team needs a dash to buoy up an already delightful experience. No matter which reality is yours, you are the one constant, as it should be.

I want to bring you back to the somewhat-gross analogy of knowing what you are spreading and leave you with wisdom from one of today's wisest management and leadership thinkers, Peter Drucker. In his classic *Harvard Business Review*

article "Managing Oneself," Drucker composes five compelling questions to answer if you want "to build a life of
excellence."

- What are my strengths?
- How do I work?
- What are my values?
- Where do I belong?
- What can I contribute?[20]

You get to leave your fingerprints on what you shape and
create at work. This includes the people you influence and
the relationships you build. Like belonging, leaving our mark
is a human drive, which urges us to make the world better. In
Drucker's widely admired article, he wisely asserts this: "Do not
try to change yourself—you are unlikely to succeed. Work to
improve the way you perform."[21] In creating belonging, leaving
your mark, and learning from those you lead, you will find
yourself changed. Sure, the doing is a bit messy. But it beats
thinking about change and not having the impact you want to
have. Action creates knowledge.

Action makes a workplace rebel.

CHAPTER 6

FALLACIES, FOES, AND TECH-FUELED FRIENDSHIPS

The Baby, the Bath Water, and Other Extreme Responses to Change

If we are to retain our humanity in the age of machines, we need to bring to the fore what it is to be human.

—Lynda Gratton

I s the quality of a virtual relationship with a colleague weaker than a relationship with someone you regularly see in person? Take the question one step further. Do your virtual employees experience belonging if they rarely or never interact with teammates in the same physical space? Despite the ubiquity of basic collaboration tools and their ability to instantly connect a team, leaders still worry about their employees' performance when working remotely. Are they *really* working? It leads to additional questions linked to performance: Can a team be high performing when everyone is not physically present? When impromptu conversations happen among employees who are located in the same physical place, are their relationships with remote employees who missed the spontaneous gathering degraded?

Scientifically speaking it is difficult to answer the above questions. But by knitting together research from neuroscience, psychology, and sociology, insights about how our brains continually evolve reveal our species' greatest strength: adapting to our environment.

A word of caution: The conclusions I lay out in the following pages are still in their infancy. Additionally, evidence about in-person team performance compared to virtual team performance still leans heavily toward "real is still the deal." As with any compelling change, there is a little drama. In this case, today's workforce expects remote working to be part of the benefits of working for you or your company. How do you integrate performance needs with expectations and even preferred ways of working? This chapter looks at these conflicting dynamics and how you can use them to support your efforts to create the experience of belonging.

ADAPTATIONS AND ADVANCES

Five years ago, when I first started studying technology's influence on relationships, much of the research posited that virtual interactions were inadequate compared to in-person interactions. The prevailing belief, backed by reputable research, still concludes that in-person, face-to-face interactions produce better results. Case in point: when customer service agents of a major bank took their breaks together, researchers from MIT learned that employee stress dropped by 19 percent, their productivity increased, and turnover dropped to 12 percent. If you have ever worked in or managed a call center, you know that these numbers are compelling. It is a high-demand environment with very structured work processes; agents are constantly monitored, and actions are measured.

The primary trigger for the compelling results was very human: people interacting with people. Though the breaks were only fifteen minutes long, the agents established a sense of camaraderie.[1] They spent the time swapping stories about work stressors and life in general. It is what we humans do. We tell stories. It is far easier to have spontaneous conversations with someone near you as opposed to launching an app and hoping to contact the person on the other side of the computer.

The underlying assumption of MIT's and others' research is that our evolutionary wiring for in-the-flesh relationships has not changed much. A contributor to this fixed brain state is the fact that the absence of physical touch, sight, or even smell interferes with quality bonding.

Our brain helps facilitate developing close ties with colleagues. When we physically interact with one another, certain triggers signal to the brain to release oxytocin. Oxytocin is a neuropeptide promoting bonding. It motivates prosocial behaviors such as trusting others, interpreting emotions in others, being generous, and building relationships.[2] Hugs, a reassuring look, or even trustworthy behaviors trigger oxytocin release.

Does the brain release oxytocin when you interact with two-dimensional teammates? In short, yes. During video meetings, for example, you can make sense of facial expressions, changes in posture, and even hear when someone's voice raises or softens. These are all triggers that tell your brain that something has changed with a person. This cues you to stop the meeting and ask your colleague what's on his mind. In short, we can develop rich relationships with virtual teammates.

When the Internet became widely available, we had little understanding of how it would change the way we interact. Studies found that social media users experienced more depression than those who abstained. The study design, however, looked at strangers observing a stranger's Facebook page. The ubiquity of the Internet now allows us to connect with family, friends, and classmates we haven't seen in decades, and even build new online relationships. We are adapting to the daily tech-tonic that soothes our need to know what our friends and connections are doing and experiencing.

Our ability to adapt to online interactions in a healthy manner was evidenced in a 2014 study from Rutgers College and the Pew Research Center. The study's focus was to measure how the Internet affects relationships. The results were wholly contradictory to earlier findings. Keith Hampton from Rutgers found that the more ways the study's participants interacted online, the more their relationships strengthened. We use social media, chat via video, email one another to share successes, losses, and even our hopes.[3] Our growing familiarity with online interactions demystifies what once was new territory. Familiarity breeds comfort and comfort is important to experiencing belonging.

While we are adapting and learning to build meaningful relationships with online colleagues, advances in technology are also helping us to create real connections with one another.

Silicon Valley CEO Peter Jackson is leading a team that is redesigning and rethinking how we collaborate technologically. Jackson's company, Bluescape, simplifies the complexities of too many collaboration tools by integrating all of them into one big interactive canvas. We all have seen the meteorologists who use big, fancy touchscreens to tell the weather's story. Imagine that screen and functionality plopped into what Bluescape calls a workspace. In that workspace (on the same screen) you have video of all your colleagues. Also on the screen is the project document the team is discussing. Jackson described to me a scenario where a team decides they need to brainstorm. In the same workspace the team uses virtual stickies and brainstorms a solution important to their project. Interacting together, moving the virtual stickies around, the team discusses and decides what they need to add to their project document.[4]

While the technology may be fascinating, it is what Jackson's company infuses with the technology that contributes to team performance and to belonging. Inclusion is a fundamental element of Bluescape. "Inclusion is where collaboration tools started," Jackson told me. "Everybody has different skills, and leveraging those can create really wonderful things." He explained that when a team "gathers" in front of a workspace, the conversations they have, the stories they tell, and the experiences they uncover are all shaping the way people connect.

"[Today] it isn't about me, me, me; it's about we, we, we," Jackson argues. He says that the collaborative dynamics of kicking around ideas, building on old ones and making them stronger, and watching and responding to how colleagues engage or disengage: these activities are central to obtaining buy-in to team decisions.[5] Technology can help teams learn to do this more effectively and reach more useful outcomes. He also notes an important truth for today's more collaborative-driven ways of working; it is not impressive when an individual crushes it. The problems your company faces cannot be solved by a superstar. They take an inclusive mindset, which requires a team who can work together. "What makes collaboration a success is inclusion and [a sense of] safety," Jacksons says.

THE INVISIBLE TECHNOLOGY

"Technology is going to get closer and closer. It's going to get invasive—we're going to wear it; it's going to be inside us. Then it's going to disappear, and we're not even going to notice it." These futuristic words are from Amy Zalman. She is the CEO of World Future Society, a futurist think tank that studies trends shaping how society will evolve.[6]

Let's pause. What was your reaction to Zalman's prognostication? I suppose for most the futuristic picture is off-putting. It is a major change, and our brain initially perceives change as a threat. One way we make sense of threats, as Zalman predicts, is by evaluating them by what we know. Most leaders do not fully understand the dynamics Zalman studies. Consequently, limited knowledge leads to a limiting pattern of thinking, and bias then clouds conclusions. In the end, the threat, which turns into biased thinking because of the absence of knowledge, leaves leaders unprepared to position their companies for the future.

Technology's invisibility may summon fears of Big Brother, a concern with merit. Humanity has a long history of disastrous temptation; the potential for misuse of technology absolutely deserves strong doses of concern and skepticism. There is still a need to define the moral and ethical boundaries associated with technology advances like machine learning, artificial intelligence, and wearables. That said, should the upsides be ignored? I don't think so. What Jackson and Zalman both envision is technology that responds to our needs.

The MIT study I mentioned earlier used special badges, which capture data showing where people gather, where pockets of disengaged employees are, and even where potential bottlenecks exist within the company's social networks. The real-time data extracted from the badges, according to Humanyze, the company that creates the technology, helps leaders improve their decisions that impact operations and the workforce.

As the advances in technology produce more and more data, companies need to rely on artificial intelligence and machine learning to make sense of the mountain of information. Buried within the ones and zeros is information that leaders could not have processed fast enough to shape workforce strategies. Now that has changed. Your company's data is now an advantage. If, for example, you can learn from the human behavior data that Humanyze provides or unite teams through Bluescape's infinite workspaces, why would you not aim these assets to improving employees' experience of work? Your competitors are. So are your colleagues.

THE RETHINKING BRAIN

Companies still have a long haul to efficiently and effectively marry technology to improve human and team interactions. I often hear from leaders and their employees that they do not like virtual team meetings. Widely available meeting and collaboration technology is awkward, clunky, and feels unnatural. Talking to a phone during a conference call hardly reflects a genuine human interaction. Some video technology is unstable making the interaction frustrating: "Mark, we can't hear you. You're on mute." These are substantial barriers to building a sense of belonging when you have remote team members.

While technology is dramatically evolving, we still have one more variable hindering geographically dispersed workers from feeling connected with one another—the brain.

Earlier I explained how oxytocin helps facilitate bonding. Researchers initially believed that virtual meetings would not positively contribute to building friendships. But we have adapted to technology's ubiquity—or more accurately, our brains have changed how they respond to human interactions.

Another musty belief is that when we reach a certain age, the brain's functionality and growth become fixed. Research from Alvaro Pascual-Leone, professor of neurology and associate dean of clinical and translational research at Harvard Medical School, reveals that the brain is in a perpetual state of plasticity: "Plasticity is an intrinsic property of the human brain and represents evolution's invention to enable the nervous system to escape the restrictions of its own genome and thus adapt to environmental pressures, physiologic changes, and experiences."[7]

Your brain is never in a resting state in terms of how it evolves in response to your world. To illustrate how quickly the brain can adapt to changing conditions, Pascual-Leone and his colleagues ran a blindfold test. Study participants were in "complete visual deprivation" for five days. Within that timeframe, the brain adapted to the temporary blindness, helping the participants recognize objects by feel alone. When the blindfold was removed, however, the region of the brain that previously helped the participants was dramatically reduced.[8]

The lesson for us non-neuroscientists is straightforward: the human brain is in a constant state of readiness and can redeploy its resources to help us function and even thrive in an endlessly changing world. As a leader, this positions an invaluable nugget of wisdom. You and your employees are quite capable of learning new ways to work. At the same time, everyone has the capacity to continue learning throughout career shifts.

These findings also shed light on how our brains can adapt to technology's influence on the way we interact. Jackson asserted that inclusion is vital for today's tech-driven workplace; this is an area where each of us can learn from those who are different from ourselves. Your rethinking brain can help you learn how to understand someone who thinks differently than you. The humanity expressed in this genuine intent to connect is transformative. We all want to contribute. It's another of our innate drives. The influence of contribution coupled with feeling wanted, valued, and welcomed is an intoxicating combination. It is also a pairing that needs to be experienced with greater frequency to exceed results and keep teams together.

THE HUMAN CHEMIST AND TEAM CHEMISTRY

There is no escaping the prevalence of bots, apps, wearables, and screens. These are de facto tools for a relevant employer. Interestingly, their increasing presence in our lives, online and offline, is having a counterintuitive effect. The frequency and duration of our time in which we "plug in" is also raising concerns about our ability to develop meaningful connections.

Concerns abound for younger generations, like Gen Y and Z, for example, who are not learning how to write with something other than a keyboard or device. It is rumored that Mark Zuckerberg, CEO of Facebook, wrote his company's owner's manual to investors, a pre-IPO communication, on his smartphone. The communication reflects the CEO's concerns and hopes linked to going public, the company's purpose, and insights about the culture and its role in generating value for shareholders. This proves that important work can be done anywhere on a multitude of devices. But despite the advantages of our highly plastic brains, too much technology has its detractions, and their effects warrant significant consideration for today's leaders.

In chapter 1, I quoted Keith Richards's view on creative alchemy: the chemistry, or hidden currents, between people that yields the greatest creations. As a human chemist responsible for orchestrating a team chemistry that yields your team's greatest creations, the intricate relationship between technology and good old-fashioned human interaction is the new leadership frontier.

The Limitations to Your Advantages

In the last few chapters I painted a basic picture of how our brains evolved to favor relationships. The size of your personal and professional network is far greater than your early ancestors'. Today, maintaining quality relationships takes time and commitment. It makes sense that technology has become central to staying in touch with others.

The other point I made is there are inherent polarities in the advantages and limitations of something good: belonging and fitting-in; in-person and virtual relationships. Just as there are limitations with too much belonging at work, human chemists need to monitor the effects of too much tech-driven interaction. Like any good chemist, leaders must know how team elements work together to avoid triggering explosions or creating a hot toxic mess. The following signs of impending trouble are linked to an imbalance between the use of technology and the frequency of bringing people together in the same physical room. At stake is the experience employees have when they believe they are valued, wanted, and welcomed. In part 3 we will examine how you can mediate the elements that just don't work together.

In Zuckerberg's owner manual he wrote that Facebook's purpose is "[To] strengthen how people relate to each other."[9] Canlis's purpose is "[To] turn people to each other." Similar intents but achieved differently, one through a digital strategy and the second via an analog method. Curiously, neither company states the value of their product or service. Instead, they communicate a desired outcome: why they make software or are in the hospitality business.

Replacing the belief that businesses are merely profit-generating machines is a more romantic business belief. People who uphold the company through commitment to a shared purpose show humanity and are rewarded in kind by a compassionate culture. A symbiotic relationship between results and relationships demands far more than managing people. Sometimes a light touch is needed, and at other times a fierce conversation is necessary to inspire performance. To know the difference is to study and practice using soft skills.

The irony does not escape me that technology could be easily classified as mechanistic. But keep in mind that this era's Fourth Industrial Revolution is marked by technological advances in genetics, nanotechnology, robotics, artificial intelligence, and even biotechnology.[10] The combining of the hard and the soft is a major theme in this new age.

Human Chemistry Lesson:
Liberation and Depletion

The consequences of too much technology in our lives has contributed to an increase in loneliness, anxiety, depression, and burnout. Technology has also widened our understanding of our place in the world, helping us to learn how other cultures live, and providing us with tools to express our ideas and creativity.

The abundance of technology contributes to information overload. In research laboratories, our consumption of online content is diminishing critical brain functions: attention, perception, decision making, and delaying gratification. Our devices are gateways to other worlds and that is leading to dysfunctions too. Dr. Adam Gazzaley, professor of neurology, psychiatry, and physiology at the University of California San Francisco, asserts that our distracted minds are minimizing positive influences on a healthy life. For example, with our faces chronically buried in our devices we are spending less time outside; devices are omnipresent at the dinner table, and we are exercising less. Our addiction to our tech is also interfering with the quality of our sleep. The dulling of our tech-addled brains is now adversely affecting the quality of relationships we have. Low-quality relationships and the absence of restorative sleep contributes to diminished capacity for empathy, collaboration, compassion, and belonging.[11]

It seems the crankier we become the faster our agency atrophies.

The ripple effect continues, unfortunately. As our social inclinations decline but our workload increases (remember we are collaborating more to get work done) we begin to experience burnout. In a 2016 report, nearly 50 percent of people say work exhausts them. The report compares the results to twenty years ago when only 18 percent of people felt burned out. It gets worse. The more burned out people feel, the more lonely they feel. One of the many benefits from feeling a sense of belonging is mitigating the experience of loneliness. Feeling alone can reduce a person's life expectancy by 70 percent.[12]

In the context of today's workplace, burnout is an epidemic. Kronos, an HR consulting firm, found in its 2017 study that 95 percent of CHROs say burnout affects employee retention. If your organization is like the many I've consulted with, then you can corroborate the other disappointing finding in the Kronos study. 87 percent of HR leaders say retention is a top priority, but 20 percent say higher priority projects prevent them from taking action.[13] It is a classic dynamic we see too often in business: build the company's growth on the backs of employees. However, this time employees' backs are bruised, broken, or just not available. A toxic contagion, burnout diminishes a company's ability to win new business by 66 percent.[14]

Burnout is attributed to a number of factors that are key to our exploration of belonging. Workload is the biggest factor. The physical work environment contributes to employees becoming unable to handle the distractions. Work schedule issues and a person's own performance round out the four major reasons for employee burnout.[15] We chat, text, and email one another long after quitting time. Since laptops and tablets are prolific in our lives, employees can work anywhere and anytime. Technology has become both a friend and foe. Our inability to know how to function, and eventually thrive, within this duality will be a barrier to shared belonging.

Wisdom for Human Chemists
in an Industrial World

The pluses and minuses of technology may have your head swiveling back and forth: Is it good? A threat? Are the issues simply magnified by overreactions and prognostications fueled by fear of the unknown?

Your response to the inevitable, the continuous integration of technology shaping how we work and live, will affect your success as a leader. In this era dubbed the Fourth Industrial Revolution, your success includes having the clarity to focus on what you can control (yourself, your response) and what you can influence (people, policy, process, decisions). The workplace issues that concern you but that you can do nothing about are a time suck and eventually become mentally exhausting.

You cannot scale back the proliferation of technology used in business today. You can, however, establish company and team practices that give employees more autonomy and freedom. Autonomy and freedom are great elixirs of agency, a person's belief that they have control over their destiny. Both technology and analog solutions will be central to guiding teams through creating a culture of belonging in a technological world. Focus on how you respond to the pluses and minuses of technology on your team's performance. Invest time in influencing company policies and expectations (spoken and unspoken) on how technology is used to connect teams. Here are some practical steps to managing technology:

- Establish a code of honor when it comes to texting, chatting, and emailing one another. Agree on when the quiet times are and how long they last. Make the exceptions to the code clear. Establish which positions, if any, are exempt from the quiet times, but establish rotation schedules to allow exempt positions time away from devices.
- Invest in technology that improves and automates scheduling employees for the best shift fit. One research firm suggests investing in a scheduling solution that can match employee skills and experiences to the right shift. The benefits are significant: less changes, predictability, and timely communication of the upcoming schedule.[16]
- Integrate technology addiction into your overall wellness education campaigns.
- Evaluate who really needs devices for work. It is a nice perk to give everyone a phone and/or a laptop. Yet what is the price you pay when an entire team is moving from fatigue to burnout?
- Examine your company's physical layout. Where can deep-work zones be created that require quiet time?
- Establish a sign or signal that alerts others to not interrupt someone.
- Evaluate the HR benefits and perks. Are there subsidies the company can provide to promote self-care? Can the vacation policy and practices be

revised to require employees to take time off beyond an extended three-day weekend? What perks would relieve employee stress—daycare, meals, car washes, meditation or nap rooms, for example?

- Redesign the way employees are brought onboard. Replace the sixteen-hour download of information that overwhelms employees with ways to boost belonging—feeling valued, wanted, and welcomed—into the onboarding experience. Develop solutions that establish connections that last beyond training. Evolve the perfunctory nature of the onboarding programs and integrate experiences of what it is like to work at your company. Include informative interactions with key employees. Quality of interactions is key.

- Establish and train everyone on meeting facilitation practices that promote psychological safety, efficiency, a bias for action, and timeliness. Limit meetings to thirty minutes. It's surprising what gets accomplished when people come prepared and there's a clear agenda dynamically facilitated.

- Celebrate intentionally. Too often work demands keep employees from having fun: back-to-back meetings, uncompromising piles of work and deadlines, client meetings and travel. You'll learn in the next section how vital play is to belonging. For now, make time to celebrate accomplishments and milestones. Their value goes beyond belonging. They are also effective ways to mitigate the deleterious effects of distress, fatigue, and burnout.

DIGITAL LIFE AND THE YEARNING
FOR SOMETHING MEANINGFUL

At the beginning of this chapter, I asked if virtual relationships can be as meaningful as those in person. Human connection, as we just examined, is adapting to our byte-shaped world. The need for human interaction, though, has always been best shaped by our ability to understand one another. To understand another person taps into the skills that make us human: empathy, listening, and collaboration, for starters.

Your success as a leader relies on using your humanity to counter the dulling effects technology has on our brains and our relationships. It may seem strange to place responsibility for tech's influence on your employees. Admittedly, I had never linked the two together until reading the research and learning from the model companies interviewed for this book. Generation Z, the youngest employees just now entering the workforce, has grown up with technology far superior to what put men on the moon. This generation's ability to discern when and how to engage with others in person or virtually relies on training from parents—and leaders once they reach the workforce. We need to coach employees to apply their humanity in developing high-quality relationships, or use what I call human-relational skills.

The use of technology without human-relational skills superficially shapes team cohesion. To inspire the experience of belonging at work, leaders and employees must reinforce the need for the ongoing development of these human-relational skills.

- Empathy to show compassion for colleagues
- Listening to understand

- Collaboration to learn to work with others
- Praise to show appreciation
- Candor to discuss differences
- Curiosity to explore ideas

Human-relational skills are not easy to train. This concerns CEOs. Eighty-eight percent have expressed that their workforce is woefully lacking in soft skills,[17] which are shaped by many influences—innate skills, education, upbringing. A workshop that shows employees how to express empathy will not immediately yield mastery. These skills are developed in many contexts throughout our lives.

Lynda Gratton, esteemed professor at the London Business School, advocates a systemic overhaul of how we shape future leaders. Per Gratton, the overhaul includes rethinking the assumptions underlying higher education.[18] Students studying business administration, for example, are taught topics that had their genesis in the first Industrial Revolution—such as running a business like a factory with little concern for the well-being of the worker. The emphasis is on the operational efficiencies of the company, strategic concepts, and HR practices that reinforce conformity and compliance. Despite the proliferation of more human-centered workplaces advocated by notable companies like Google, The Container Store, Canlis Restaurant, Barry-Wehmiller, and LinkedIn, higher education is behind in shaping soft skills in future leaders of business.

But higher education is not the only way in which human-relational skills are taught. You have significant influence on your employees' experience of work. The expectations you have for your team and how they interact, communicate, and problem solve are excellent ways to coach and reinforce soft skills. This growth can happen on the job as well as through professional development opportunities.

The concern that automation, machine learning, virtual reality, and artificial intelligence will replace humans has been overstated. The delicacy needed to apply the soft skills discussed above requires something a machine cannot effectively do, at least for now: discern and make sense of nuances in human behavior or make decisions that cannot rely solely on data and algorithms. Where machines rely on the Internet and programs to function and perform actions per their codes, our experiences color our understanding of a complicated world.

As automation gobbles up more mundane tasks that we do not want or need to do, humans will be redirected to solve complex, sometimes wicked problems. Working alongside people takes more than technical or professional skills. Your knowledge of how to relate with others and collaborate to achieve desired outcomes will be critical for the success of you and your team.

It has always been a brave new world. We have always been moving towards some new world where society and technology influence how we work and live. While the dystopian scenarios, like that in Aldous Huxley's book *Brave New World,* can evoke both curiosity and depression at the same time, how you personally respond to the emphatic march of modernization will determine your success and even your well-being.

None of us want to be left behind. As I've stated and restated throughout this book, our human nature is driven by polarities that have kept our species alive: curiosity and fear; working together and needing alone time, for starters. These are powerful drivers that shape how we experience life. Therefore, they are also powerful drivers on how you lead and shape your employees' experience of work. Technology and its progressive reach is nearly unstoppable. The leaders who will have the biggest impact, or make a dent in the universe as Steve Jobs advocated, are the ones who can adapt to the blurring of AI and human experience.

Resistance to progress is futile.

It is essential for every leader—formal or informal, in every company—to adapt to the changing environment and give their people opportunities to feel valued and contribute to work and society in meaningful ways.

PART III

UNIFYING YOUR TRIBE

CHAPTER 7

FEELING VALUED

The Astonishing Acts of
Company Evangelists

When you're a carpenter making a beautiful chest of drawers, you're not going to use a piece of plywood on the back, even though it faces the wall and nobody will ever see it. You'll know it's there; so, you're going to use a beautiful piece of wood on the back.

—Steve Jobs on craftsmanship

I often think that I romanticize work. But upon reflection, it is not work that I'm romanticizing; it's the craft it takes to do outstanding work. Think about what you experience when you watch your favorite athlete or someone really good at what they do. I love observing and learning from people who clearly knows their profession's practices, methods, and, equally as important, can use finesse when interacting with others. Steve Jobs's quote at the top of this chapter zeros in on the nuances of craftsmanship—attention to detail and putting in the time to create something beautiful and useful.

We all have the capacity to hone what we do and cultivate our craft. A line cook in a restaurant shows his craft by developing a keen awareness of what is happening at all times in the kitchen. A professional salesperson knows when and how to adjust interactions with a hesitant potential customer. An engineer codes meticulously, avoiding shortcuts, so that the software does what it is supposed to do. Your employees' craftsmanship is a collection of innate behavior and learned skills that contribute to astonishing work.

To become aware of these invisible influences on performance, it is critical to cultivate a habit of curiosity. An employee's curiosity to learn the nuances of a craft must be treated with the utmost respect. It needs to be encouraged—and required—in any team seeking astonishing results. To help facilitate and reinforce the refinement of one's craft, a fundamental human need must be experienced—feeling valued.

Without feeling valued by our coworkers, the story we tell through our performance will be disappointing. Without feeling valued, we leave our gumption, passion, and commitment behind. Not one of us shows up to work enthusiastic when our contributions go unacknowledged. Work remains a list of routine tasks to be completed. Teams failing to create a work environment that taps into employees' craftsmanship miss out on the benefits of employees deeply satisfied from doing the work to be great.

A SENSE OF PLACE

"This place and these people are home to us." Taken from Canlis's website, this quote embodies all that Bruce and I learned from spending time at the famed restaurant. Belonging is rooted in identifying with a physical place. Some Native American tribes believe that knowing the land through the four seasons creates a sense of place, a connection between person and land. This belief creates a tradition that connects the members of a tribe.

A shared belief system turns a vast landscape into something of importance. A tribe's reverence for the land, and their shared practices to honor it, intensify the hidden currents between the people and the land. A place becomes more than a location. It becomes sacred. It shapes identity and relationships. A sense of place prioritizes what matters most.

At Canlis, a sense of place means being in relationships—with guests, family members, and team members. Sharing a meal together is a deeply symbolic gesture that says you belong. Each evening before the guests arrive, the team working that night eats together. While they eat, they learn about that night's guest list. This tradition imbues connection among the employees, marking the place called Canlis. And when that identifier evokes positive memories—the sounds of conversations, the smells of food—the workplace becomes a sacred place. It is the place where everyone working that night is unified in a simple purpose: bring people together. Their reverence for the workplace and their guests feels respectful. A sense of ownership colors how Canlis employees treat the space in the restaurant. What you put in is what you get in return. For example, every employee—regardless of seniority level—stops in their tracks when a guest walks by. The simple gesture is an act of respect, perhaps even deference. The intention to always stop for guests is but one way the place called Canlis becomes special, memorable—a place where guests want to return. Going one step further, this place becomes one where employees also want to return.

My worry about over-romanticizing work seems silly when I replay in my mind the dedication Canlis employees show in creating an unforgettable experience for guests. What Bruce and I witnessed was not a perfunctory display of work. It was an intentional, unified effort by a group of people who felt valued. They demonstrated it by brilliant displays in their respective crafts. Canlis is indeed a place that comes to life by traditions and the relationships between people who honor them.

To believe that we are right where we need to be and to feel valued has a calming influence on how we work. Hunter Powell, a principal in one of Barry-Wehmiller's companies, observed the significant influence of feeling valued: "Let people flourish in their own way. I think it's so easy for a leader of people to impose their will [and push employees to do things] their way."[1] Powell's word choice, flourish, is important. Flourishing is a deeper experience related to well-being and a life well-lived. Having peers and even your boss express how much they appreciate your contribution helps connect you to the workplace. It enriches your relationships. It influences your craft. Are these not invaluable outcomes if you want a team to achieve results that astonish and delight?

EXPRESSLY APPRECIATED

So what does feeling valued mean? From our interviews with employees, it comes down to expressly communicating appreciation for the contribution, effort, and sacrifices employees make to do great work. A word of caution though: don't confuse feeling valued with being coddled. High performers and high-performance teams need reminding that they are valued. If you ask these employees if they need the adulations, they typically say it is unnecessary. Do not believe it. It is human to like praise. The nuance is in how you deliver it. Notice, however, that there is another component to feeling valued—sacrifice.

More and more, the work today's employees put into their craft is not restricted to traditional work hours. In start-ups, working on weekends is often necessary to get a product to market. In a peak retail season such as Christmas, longer hours are needed, and employees have less time to be with family and friends. Or perhaps you decide it is best to stay quiet on an issue important to you because the timing isn't right. We all make sacrifices for the greater good. Acknowledge when employees put the company's or team's interests over their family or personal life. It costs you nothing and is invaluable when genuinely communicated.

When You Are So Good You Become
the Voice of an Alien Race

There is a famous tuba player at the University of Southern California. This tuba player is so revered that Josh Groban, Barbra

Streisand, and Frank Sinatra (to name but a few stars) have recorded albums with him. His tuba is the "Voice of the Mothership" in *Close Encounters of the Third Kind*. Jim Self, an adjunct professor at USC Thornton School of Music, has excelled in contributing to great musical collaborations.[2] When I spoke with Self, his accolades seemed to have only deepened his humility.

"You don't survive in the freelance world if you're an a-hole," Self said to me over the phone. He was referring to the chemistry between musicians. Tuba players are supporting cast members in an orchestra. It is rare (except when the tuba is the voice of an alien race) that this big and seemingly awkward instrument gets a solo in a musical composition. For a tuba player to assert himself unnecessarily as the lead instrument will only infuriate the other musicians. A musical piece is comprised of many instruments, and to believe your instrument is more important than the whole of the composition, well, such a belief feeds the "a-hole" description Self mentioned.[3]

Despite the supporting role tuba players have, Self has made it part of his invaluable contribution to movies and recordings. What he brings to a collaboration is not a prima donna mentality but a cohesive mindset. "We get into each other's sounds," he told me.[4] You may not be a musician or consider yourself a creative, but you can probably still understand the poetics in his words. For Jim Self to get into the sounds of his fellow musicians requires patience and sacrifice. He knows when to listen and watch what the others are doing. He also knows when to refrain from playing to allow another musician to have his or her moment. Finally, he knows which note to play and its timbre to produce the desired, collective sound. To play well with others, Self must know when to follow, lead, and wait.

Musicians practice with one another and give feedback to improve their performance. A tight-knit group, no matter the genre of music, can delight audiences, which is not very different from what your team produces together. When musicians know their value, they make great music. When each person on your team knows his or her value, the team creates inspiring results.

This greatness, however, is best achieved when the talents and ideas that each person contributes, and the sacrifices made are acknowledged and appreciated . . . repeatedly. This is not groundbreaking news. Research has continuously revealed how important recognition and praise is to performance and employee morale. I'm simply connecting their significance to its influence on belonging.

The difference, however, is a heavy emphasis on a *collective* performance. If a musician doesn't practice, then his contribution will be subpar. No great symphony creates music that gives people chills if they do not work together and if each musician doesn't practice on his or her own. This dynamic interplay between practice and team performance was quite pronounced at Canlis.

One of the servers, Amanda Lynn Sullivan, shared stories about how the team would practice together by reflecting on how the night's service went. Restaurants are very fluid environments. Mistakes are made in preparing food or mixing the cocktail to the guest's specifications. Various teams meet after hours to discuss how each night went. They dissect problems and find solutions without the encouragement of management. The team then propagates the solution to others, so the problem does not continue.[5]

Let's pause here for a moment. You may be tempted to dismiss these examples as obvious. Ask yourself, though, would the initiative Sullivan and her colleagues demonstrate occur if they did not feel valued? The short answer is no. This is the penultimate outcome from feeling valued at work. When you recognize the talents or the potential talent in your employees and team and expressly communicate that you appreciate their contributions and sacrifices, it reduces or eliminates a destructive internal dialogue: "Nobody notices the hard work I put in." "Management gets all the glory and we work our asses off and get no recognition." I said it earlier: It is human to want to be recognized. In the absence of feeling valued, people will come to conclusions about their performance. You will not like what they decide.

Praise, however, is but one part of showing that you value your people. Money is another way. At The Container Store, they pay about twice the wage that is common for the retail industry. "We get three times the productivity and only two times the cost," Kip Tindell tells me. "When employees believe they are treated fairly and feel like they have a piece of the action," they want to do their best work.[6]

It has been said that Michelangelo did not create his most-famous sculpture; he merely released David from within that beautiful piece of marble. Who are the Michelangelos on your team? Who are the Davids on your team who merely need someone to help them reveal their value? How can you express to both groups how much you value their craftsmanship? Greatness is shaped by our relationships. How do your relationships unleash the Michelangelos on your team? Additionally, how do you express that employees are valued members of your team?

THE EXPERIENCE OF BELONGING AT WORK FRAMEWORK

For employees to feel valued at work it takes more than encouragement and recognition. The experience at work also needs to signal that they are valued. Words are one thing; experience is altogether something different and more powerful.

Experiences are not only emotionally evocative, but we remember them longer than words or gifts. When positive emotions, like those from belonging, shape experiences something important occurs in our brains that positions us to perform at higher levels.

Researchers continue to deepen our understanding of how the hippocampus helps make experiences "sticky" in our memories. It's a small organ that is part of our limbic system, which regulates how we processes emotions. When we experience positive emotions, like those that we feel from a sense of belonging, our brain is primed to help us perform better. Think of the two, our brain and positive experiences, as jet fuel for our performance. A person's cognitive abilities and the resultant actions are broadened. Growing empirical evidence also finds that positive emotions boost creativity, willingness to participate in new experiences, and even receive constructive feedback.

Think of the above benefits of positivity as personally beneficial. The advantages are also extended to our friends. When our brains are primed by emotions like joy or satisfaction, we are naturally driven to establish and maintain social connections. Thus, belonging becomes one of many beneficial biological outcomes that help us thrive, rise above the stressors of life, and, ultimately, have a greater cognitive capacity to perform.[7]

If people associate feeling valued with their work because their experience is mostly positive, it helps them develop positive associations. Thus they are positioned to cognitively outperform peers who have a negative experience.[8] Negative experiences interfere with the hippocampus's function. Consequently, the amygdala, the oldest part of our brain associated with fear responses, processes the negative experience in a fight-or-flight mode. Our brain then sends us down a narrow-focus path leading to self-preservation and defensive behaviors, for example.[9]

Let's pull the brain science out of research and put it into the workplace. When you show employees they are valued, their positive emotions prime them to experience a sense of belonging in your team and even in the company. Naturally, the emotions will vary between employees. You simply want to be a catalyst for them to benefit from a positive experience.

Unfortunately more than three-quarters of the US workforce have a negative experience.[10] When employees work with fear, chronic stress levels, and frustrations, the amygdala hijacks the possibility of a great experience. Feeling valued is an unlikely conclusion in this context.

You do not need to be a brain doctor to influence belonging experiences. In fact, the balance of this book will show you how to tap into the surprising secret to high performance, astonishing results, and a cohesive team in the face of negative experiences.

How to Help Employees
Experience Belonging at Work

Figures 7.1 and 7.2 show the full framework for influencing belonging at work. This includes what happens when any one or two of the experiences is absent. I list the definitions and inputs to help you understand the framework, and chapters 8 and 9 will dive deep into each belonging experience.

- Feeling valued is associated with employees' talents and strengths. Talents are "what the employee is capable of doing or learning." Strengths are "the categories of work that energize the employee": strategic thinking, being creative, analytical work, or planning.
- Feeling wanted is defined as "my boss and the organization care about me as a human being." It is associated with being known and respected. Being known is "acknowledging with interest the whole person and not focusing only on the employee identity." Employees are not just a head count. They are human beings with lives that sometime are predictable and other times are chaotic. Respect is predominately about acknowledging and honoring differences: gender, sexual orientation, race, ways of thinking, experience levels.
- Feeling welcome is defined as "I have a place in the team." It is associated with psychological safety. Imagine being in a meeting with colleagues. You have a perspective contrary to the dominant one. If you feel

that contrarian beliefs are openly encouraged and explored, psychological safety is high. If, however, you have experienced through your own actions or those of another that different ideas are not welcome, then the environment may not feel psychologically safe.

- No one belonging experience is more important than another. Their alchemy is what matters. Together they all help you and your employees experience belonging at work. If one or two experiences are absent, the outcomes are suboptimal regarding performance, results, and team dynamics. If you feel that your effort is valued and people care about you (feeling wanted), but you do not experience feeling welcomed, your place in the team may come with conditions or fitting in is reinforced.

FIGURE 7.1

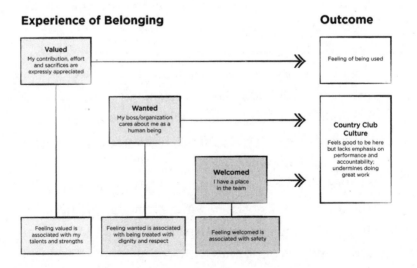

Experience of Belonging   Outcome

| Valued | | |
| My contribution, effort and sacrifices are expressly appreciated | | Feeling of being used |

	Wanted	
	My boss/organization cares about me as a human being	Country Club Culture
		Feels good to be here but lacks emphasis on performance and accountability; undermines doing great work

| | | Welcomed |
| | | I have a place in the team |

| Feeling valued is associated with my talents and strengths | Feeling wanted is associated with being treated with dignity and respect | Feeling welcomed is associated with safety |

FIGURE 7.2

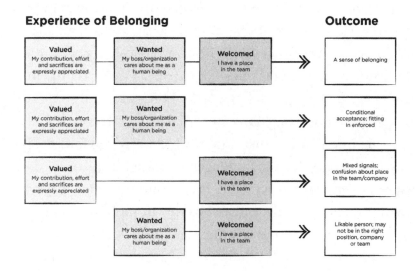

Experience of Belonging   **Outcome**

Valued — My contribution, effort and sacrifices are expressly appreciated	Wanted — My boss/organization cares about me as a human being	Welcomed — I have a place in the team	A sense of belonging
Valued — My contribution, effort and sacrifices are expressly appreciated	Wanted — My boss/organization cares about me as a human being		Conditional acceptance; fitting in enforced
Valued — My contribution, effort and sacrifices are expressly appreciated		Welcomed — I have a place in the team	Mixed signals; confusion about place in the team/company
	Wanted — My boss/organization cares about me as a human being	Welcomed — I have a place in the team	Likable person; may not be in the right position, company or team

Likeable but Not Valued

When feeling valued by the boss or by the company is absent, but the employee feels wanted and welcomed, the result is flat-out frustrating. The employee is not the only one frustrated; so are his colleagues.

In government, it is common practice to promote people into management who are not ready for the responsibility. One of my former clients promoted an analyst into a management role. The employee's new responsibilities were deeply linked to organizational development (OD) skills. OD practitioners are highly skilled and operate in a highly professionalized capacity. In the case of my client, the promoted analyst had some exposure to OD concepts; however, he did not have the depth in skills needed to help the organization. He received the promotion, in part, because the company believed in him (feeling wanted). He was initially included in important management meetings (feeling welcomed). Unfortunately, his underdeveloped OD skills became apparent in his results.

The constructive feedback he continuously received did not lead to significant behavior change. Concurrently, his team became frustrated at the lack of direction and support. A negative reinforcing loop emerged. Weak professional skills deepened everyone's frustrations, which only reinforced his lack of feeling valued. The longer he stayed in his role, the worse he felt. He was a likable man, even fun to be around. But the absence of skills and an inability to apply his strengths merely revealed he was not in the right position. Most will not experience belonging when they do not receive recognition for their work or for the sacrifices made. They could feel as though they are being taken advantage of by their employer. And some are oblivious about the mismatch altogether.

The belonging experience is not always positive. Work realities are often a mix of positive and infuriating events. The true test to reinforce the belonging experience in the ups-and-downs of work life is to consistently lead from the three belonging experiences. In chapter 11 you will find the leadership code that feeds into belonging at work. But first, let's look at the essential inputs that support employees' sense of feeling valued.

UNLEASH YOUR EMPLOYEE EVANGELISTS

At LinkedIn, belonging is core to the company's culture. Unlike any of the other companies we studied, LinkedIn is figuring out how to operationalize belonging. In a hip meeting room encased in glass, Bruce and I meet with the Diversity, Inclusion, and Belonging (DIB) team. The team has myriad responsibilities, from measuring the outcomes of their programs to rolling out learning solutions that help the DIBs team evangelize the personal and business value of feeling valued, wanted, and welcomed.

One program that is central to LinkedIn's culture of belonging is Innovation Day, or InDay. It's a day where employees invest in themselves, but it is often a selfless expression to help others. Each monthly InDay has a theme and is observed throughout the company's locations. On the day we met the DIBs team, it was an InDay. The focus was giving back to the community. Some employees in the San Francisco office went into the nearby neighborhoods to connect with and help the homeless.[11]

Feeling valued is a powerful influence on bone-deep pride; pride is a powerful motivator to evangelism. Evangelism in this context is not about religion. The original Greek meaning of evangelize is "to share good news." In that context, when employees willingly participate in the company's culture, the good news they spread is that people do care and do want to help those in need. It is hard to not feel a kindred connection with colleagues when helping others. The shared experience builds and deepens relationships.

Employee evangelists rarely need to be asked to share why they love working for the company. However, the belonging is not the only trigger for employees to proactively show their pride for your company. In terms of belonging and the experience of feeling valued, there is little surprise as to what evokes feeling valued. When we sifted through our interview data, we found the following themes emerge in all the model companies.

Theme I:
The People Make All the Difference

It isn't rocket science to connect the importance of high-quality relationships to feeling valued. Through the stories employees and people leaders shared with us, it was evident that telling and showing employees that their investment in time at work is valued is deeply motivating. Colleagues who spend time together—inside and outside of work—build a deeper connection with one another. We heard repeatedly "The people I work with make the sacrifice worth it." We call the type of relationship that leads to belonging high resonant relationships.

The word *resonance* has symbolic meaning to relationships. In music, resonance helps harmonize each guitar's vibrations: our team harmonizes its talents effectively. Televisions rely on electrical resonance to display different channels: we blend our skills to deliver value to multiple people. Resonance in relationships provides stability. It helps unify our differences in an effective manner. If you recall from chapter 1, I used the analogy of hidden currents between people. In highly resonant relationships, the hidden currents help teams better work together. Therefore, highly resonant relationships harmonize people's talents and traits to a desirable outcome. This is a complimentary resonance.

As in nature, there is always a counter force to a favorable force. The same is true with the relationships we have with colleagues. The counter force to complimentary resonance is destructive resonance, which causes instability and subpar outcomes. Dysfunctional dynamics prevent across-the-board team cohesion. Factions can form within the team, resulting in friction. The friction degrades the quality of the team's output.

Somewhere between complimentary and destructive resonance is weak resonance, when little effort has been made to create shared experiences. The team may be new and not yet had a struggle to overcome. Or, like in most American companies, there is a lopsided emphasis on individual contributions and lots of lip service to the importance of teamwork. Weak resonant relationships have some positive charge: people are cordial and friendly, but they claim to be too busy to spend time with one another in a nonwork context.

At Canlis, the people leaders and employees constantly used the phrase "people want to be heard." For the teams at Canlis, this means making time to hear other perspective, ideas, and even stories. The emphasis is on connection rather than a contractual arrangement to do a job.

Theme 2:
People Want to Be Seen

To help others feel valued means genuinely listening to their ideas, even if they challenge your own thinking. Similarly, acknowledging people for who they are and what they bring to the team is essential. Rhonda Spencer, Barry-Wehmiller's chief people officer, shared with me a story of "being seen."

Early in her career, a more senior leader recognized Rhonda's talents. Those talents were in Rhonda's blind spots. So the senior leader intentionally spent time with her and helped her look into those blind spots. Rhonda learned that she had something to offer. As she told me, "I became fearless and fierce [in my performance]."

We cannot be sideline leaders. Leaders are hands-on. And when you or any other leader steps up to coach, encourage, and have the difficult conversations, employees feel valued because they are seen. When employees are seen, they know they are not working hard to benefit senior managers. They are working hard for a purpose.

Employee evangelists are self-identified. They speak up about working for you because they feel valued. You don't need to ask them to write a positive company review on Glassdoor, or to promote the company's product in a blog post on LinkedIn. Employees do it because of their bone-deep pride.

CHAPTER 8

FEELING WANTED

Employees Are Not
Fools or Pigs

Our lives are measured in moments, and defining moments
are the ones that endure in our memories.

—Chip and Dan Heath,
The Power of Moments

A woman's place is in the resistance," read the signs at the
2017 Women's March. The words were superimposed
over an iconic picture of Princess Leia from the early
Star Wars films. More recently she has been labeled the Hutt-
slayer.[1] Carrie Fisher has long been an inspiration for women
who fight for equality. Fisher's passing pushed her influence
to the forefront at the 2017 Women's March. The #MeToo

movement and the current political agendas had also shined a glaring light on the fact that gender equality hadn't made as much progress as we wanted to believe.

Always a reflection of what's happening in society, organizations in 2017 were also struggling to recover from outmoded beliefs and practices; an unrelenting storyline of men sexually harassing women; gender pay inequality; and debate on when to dip its toe in the divisive political discourse. In America and countries around the globe, a toxic theme dominated social and workplace trends—fit in, shut up, or be cast out. But redemption has a way of helping release those caught in the nets of someone else's ignorance and stupidity. It helps find justice and, hopefully, a path to healing.

No matter the social context, when any of us do not feel wanted, unrest ensues. Self-doubt, anger, and disappointment replace progress and growth. Our need to protect ourselves when we don't believe we are wanted thrusts us into survival mode. Our amygdala kicks into high gear, triggering cortisol to drive us to fight or flee from whatever is making us feel unsafe. The cortisol induces a state of stress and anxiety, interfering with our desires to establish resonate relationships. Cognition is impaired. Creativity is curbed. Nothing positive comes from worrying about being accepted for who you are and what you bring to a team. In companies that fail to create belonging, somewhere are culpable managers who ignored or gave up responsibility for creating a positive work environment.

Feeling wanted is inextricably linked to our work friendships and how we view our place in the team. For this reason, the absence of resonate relationships cuts deeper than not feeling valued or welcomed. The stronger the bonds between friends, the more cared for we feel. The more at ease we feel. We feel more known. It is the comfort of being known that makes this particular experience of belonging so powerful. When friendships are meaningful, we feel better about ourselves. And when they are absent or too dysfunctional, we find the company of misery too comforting.

Not only do we spend more time at work compared to other social situations, we also feel proud when we do great work. Work occupies our thoughts. It is a major part of our conversations with friends and family. It is an expression of our individual contribution to something outside ourselves. When we feel cared about, we feel freer to explore and express our talents. We find acceptance from the relationships that shape the biggest part of our day. This is deeply satisfying to our need to belong.

As leaders, we can no longer believe that work is business. Work is identity. It is how we make sense of a big part of our lives. This may be positive: "I work because I want to make a difference." "I look at my work as my calling." "I save lives." Or it may be negative: "I have nothing left to give my family after a day of work." "My boss has no clue how his wishy-washy style slows me down." "I hate my job." You get to be part of this life-shaping experience. It will never be all pleasure; it's a little like that James Taylor song "Fire and Rain": a little bit of fire and a little bit of rain.

It is in the totality of the experience called belonging that those you lead believe working with you is a career highlight. Unfortunately, the opposite can also be true. While feeling wanted is not more important than the other two belonging experiences, its absence cuts more deeply.

BETTER TO NOT BE A FOOL OR A PIG

Are there moral implications if a leader fails to address an issue that undermines his team's work? Or asked pointedly, what responsibility does a leader have when his actions and words negatively affect employees' well-being? Success? Organizational growth? Raving fans of your service or product? Philosopher John Stuart Mill might simply answer these questions with a resolute "Yes."

In the nineteenth century Mill was a persuasive voice in British social and political discourse. He asserted that we make choices based on their utility, our response to the pleasure or pain we experience as a result of our decision. But despite the possibility of pain, Mill believed we make the best decision based on what is right for the greater good. This may seem an absurd assertion given our current political, social, and even environmental scandals. Clearly, we have not made the best decisions by calling upon our higher selves and doing what is best for the greater good. This, to Mill, would mean we have not learned from our collective experiences. Thus, he might see us as fools. For Mill, fools are those who do not learn from their past experiences. Additionally, those who apply new insights to help understand and resolve a problem would be of a higher character. A person with upstanding character acts in the best interest of the greater good. In contrast, to act in self-interest would make you a pig, according to Mill's famous comparison.[2] He did not mean this in a pejorative way. A pig is a base animal not fully aware of its character or impact on others.[3]

When you look back over the course of your career, which events were better understood after hearing a different perspective from a trusted confidant? As you scan your past to the present day, which decisions did you make that truly were in the best interest of the greater good? I don't ask these questions to convict or convince you. They serve as a reminder for all of us that we are imperfect. We will continue to accommodate our bias's influence over our actions and judgments. We will always be tempted to avoid painful realizations and truths. What you learn from mistakes and how you apply those lessons makes the difference.

Work today is not what it used to be. This is for the betterment of employees, customers, shareholders, and stakeholders. But none of us can deliver the value customers expect by doing what we have always done. Researchers across many disciplines have broadened our awareness and understanding of topics such as utility and belonging. I know that you are not a fool or a pig. You clearly see the value in tapping into different ways to help your company succeed.

One of those ways is understanding the role that experiences play in performance, in commitment to excellent work, and ultimately in shaping the experience of work through belonging, which includes showing employees they are wanted.

A powerful influence on feeling wanted is the moments and experiences employees have while working at your company. There are important nuances to effectively designing these. For example, why do some experiences stick with us? And which memories are less influenced by our biases?

MICRO-MOMENTS AND LONGER EXPERIENCES

For our purposes, moments and experiences are mostly synonymous in their outcome: memorable experiences that are associated with strong emotions (Mill's pleasure and pain, for example). I do make a distinction, however, between the two terms. Firstly, micro-moments are brief interactions that can be planned or occur at random. These interactions—checking in with the team to see how their weekend was, for example—occur in real time. There is little to no preparation in a micro-moment. Second, longer experiences are intentionally designed to elicit emotions that make them so memorable that their influence lingers long after the interaction. As an example, a longer experience at Barry-Wehmiller would be getting to drive a luxury car for a week. At Canlis it could be giving an employee time off to prepare for a career-changing test. Or at LinkedIn, it can be the pride in reflecting on all the good things done during InDays.

Relying on the totality of micro-moments and longer experiences contributes to what psychologists and economists call *experienced utility*. Experienced utility colors our understanding over time. It also shapes our current and future actions.

For example, you eagerly anticipate the annual sales kickoff meeting. As soon as you can, you make your travel plans, eager for two days of time well spent. You recall the meetings to always be high energy, feature an inspiring speaker, and provide time with friends and colleagues—a rare treat. The positive emotions you feel about the annual meeting accumulate over time. They lead to highly desirable behaviors: talking up the event with colleagues or new hires, proudly sharing with friends or online how awesome the company is, or even making future financial plans because you want to stay with the company.

The experience of feeling wanted is influenced by micro-moments and experiences. Though my examples have been positive, experienced utility also reflects painful emotions. For example, let's say you do not get the promotion you wanted. The hiring manager told you that you needed a few more years' experience in your current role. While disappointing, you appreciated the candid feedback. Associated with this experience is the intensity of disappointment. I'll expand on why this is important in the next section. For now, know that painful experiences can be positive memories.

The time we spend at work is shaped by countless interactions. Micro-moments and longer experiences help us pluck from the innumerable interactions those that matter. When you intentionally shape employees' experiences, you positively influence their emotions. This becomes key for belonging at work. It is also an impactful way of showing you care, know, and respect your employees.

The Nucleus to Making
Moments That Matter

My sister-in-law loves to give experiences as gifts. For Christmas we received a date-night package: dinner at a nice restaurant and fun at Topgolf. She believes, and you will soon see that research agrees with her, that we will remember and cherish the experiential gift longer than receiving a sweater or socks or electronics.

Why would a family member care about how I respond to a gift exchange? It is a common, sometimes annual ritual, after all. The answer is central to the understanding of belonging at work: happiness.

By *happiness*, I am referring to the deeply fulfilling emotions that come from living a fulfilling life. Given that we spend more than a third of our time working, happiness from our career also contributes to a life we want. As part of our survival instinct, we seek to maximize living our own version of the good life. This is not to say we want to experience only pleasurable events. Remember, Mill's argument about utility reinforced that our character is also informed by painful events.

The past, the present, and the future shape the meaning of our experiences. Embedded in those moments are conclusions you've made. You give meaning to those moments and experiences, but you don't remember every single one. Researchers have learned that what helps us remember the good, the bad, and the ugly are two important moments in an experience—the peak and the ending moments. This is more commonly known as the peak–end rule.

Barbara Fredrickson, whose research was mentioned in chapter 3, has studied peaks and ending moments. In fact, she coined the phrase *peak–end rule* based on years of research. Fredrickson, along with many other notable researchers, has built on John Stuart Mill's work on utility. A cast of notable, even Noble Prize–winning experts are deepening our understanding of how experiences shape our decisions, why some experiences stick with us, and why some do not.

The peak–end rule states that we place greatest importance on the beginning of an experience, an intense moment, and the ending.[4] According to Fredrickson, "People's past and ongoing affective experiences guide their decisions about the future." She says that we evaluate experiences based on the emotions we feel at the time, our mood, and even our hopes and dreads are factors. Fredrickson concludes that the choices we make about an experience are linked to our future happiness.[5] This is where Mill's point about learning from the past becomes important. If we don't learn from our past mistakes, we are likely to repeat the same faulty choices.

In the companies I have studied or consulted with, and the thousands of leaders I've taught or spoken with at keynotes and workshops, I hear countless stories of intense moments at work. Some stories are great, some astonishingly sad, and others everything in between. Whether you've thought about experiences in the workplace or not, they are occurring. The question is are you intentionally influencing them? Or does a collection of unorchestrated experiences degrade work and belonging? No great company culture and workplace climate evolve without intention.

Before we look at how to tie the science of experiences to practical belonging strategies, here are a few more useful research findings linked to the peak–end rule:

- Peaks and endings stand out in our memories because of the personal meaning we attribute to them.
- Peak effects are not always pleasurable. In one of Fredrickson's studies, students each plunged a hand into 14°C water for sixty seconds. In the second trial, the students plunged their hands back into the same agonizingly cold water for sixty seconds. Then, for an additional thirty seconds with the same hand in the water, the temperature was raised to 15°C. Afterward the students were asked which trial they would repeat. Sixty-nine percent preferred the longer trial. Why? According the Fredrickson, "Participants would retain a more favorable memory of the longer trial because it ended with a lower level of pain." In other similarly designed trials, participants repeatedly chose the second, longer time period because it was less painful than the first trial. Keep in mind that the peak–end rule predicts that we remember peak moments and endings more than any other memory.
- Employees' global understanding of their own peak and ending experiences reduces the level of bias common in recalling the past. The reason for

this is probably not surprising: we remember the peaks and endings more clearly because they are important to us.

- When we evaluate and draw conclusions about an experience, our brain recalls the totality of the peaks and endings. Retrospectively, we are evaluating if the experience is something we want to continue, recommend to others, spur us to seek similar experiences, or just end.
- We prioritize spending time with people important to us when we anticipate the relationship coming to an end.[6]
- Pleasure and pain are not directly felt; they are responses to the experience.[7]

With science on your side and practical business experience, too, you and your company can leverage the brain science to create meaningful moments for employees (see Table 8.1). Experiences can be micro-moment, when an employee challenges the status quo and it leads to a great discussion, for example. Longer experiences could be an employee being selected to lead a highly visible, important project that was important to him or her. Experiences can be grand gestures or small ones, organizationally implemented or enacted at the team level.

Since experiences are shaped by personal relevance, showing employees they are cared about, known, and respected is a powerhouse for shaping belonging at work. Who is central to feeling wanted?

TABLE 8.1: EXPERIENCE STRATEGIES

Elements for Experiences	Experience Strategies
"Anticipation" The key is that the experience is widely known and generates positive emotions.	Develop an end-to-end onboarding experience that begins before an employee's first day. Establish celebrations associated with important milestones: retirement, goal achievement, tours of duty, promotions, peer recognition.
"I Want to Feel Something" Tap into how positive and negative emotions influence experiences. Barbara Fredrickson recommends focusing on emotions that are equated with high meaning. In other words, emotional responses that money cannot influence.	Incorporate play to promote camaraderie, connection, even break down barriers. Establish a program that captures live customer testimonies about how employees' hard work made an impact. Volunteer as a team. Implement programs that promote skip-level mentorships—a vice president mentoring a new manager, for example. Organize programs and events that help employees establish resonate relationships.
"Elegant Endings" Research shows that when an experience comes to an end, its memorability is heightened, suggesting endings carry more cognitive importance than beginnings or peak moments.	Develop services or programs that help difficult events end with a positive look to the future. Create an alumni program that allows people who leave the company to have access to alumni perks: benefits, access to special events, etc.

When Feeling Wanted Fails

The experience of belonging centers on whether you believe your boss cares about you as a human being. When that belief is absent, a basic human need goes unmet. The psychological effects are damaging.

- Increased likelihood of depression
- Unhealthy levels of stress or distress
- Less happiness
- Lower satisfaction with friendships and relationships
- Negative impact on a meaningful existence[8]

We don't develop our desire to connect with and be wanted by other human beings. This human need is encoded in us. When children are denied the connection from feeling wanted by their mothers, psychogenic dwarfism can develop. Psychogenic dwarfism is a growth disorder that medical professionals have determined is caused, in large part, by emotional stress and the deprivation of positive emotions between child and mother. The stress affects the central nervous system causing "marked retardation of growth, hormonal changes (Gh, somatomedin, and cortisol), and behavioral changes."[9] Poet Emily Dickinson wrote "the heart wants what it wants." Though often attributed to romantic love and attraction, the message is universal. When we are denied attention, damaging effects to our health are unavoidable.

In our model companies, we repeatedly heard stories about expressions of feeling wanted. When you read the examples below, evaluate how "feeling wanted" is interpreted. The main components of experiences that signal to employees that they are wanted are "I am known and respected." These two outcomes of feeling wanted can take many different forms.

Sometimes, after the last guests have left Canlis, employees break into teams and play laser tag inside and outside the restaurant. Play becomes an expression of feeling wanted.[10]

At Barry-Wehmiller, senior content strategist Brent Stewart shared a sentimental and thoughtful "I am wanted" story. After Brent's wedding, his team decorated his cube in a Hawaiian theme, the location of his then-upcoming honeymoon. What made this a meaningful experience was how the team incorporated pictures into their decorations. They combed through his Facebook page and printed pictures from Brent's wedding day. Their thoughtfulness was so significant to Brent that three months later he had not taken down the decorations, including the hula skirt around his desk chair.[11]

How do you show your employees that they are wanted? Perhaps the most meaningful way to show how much you know and respect them is by paying attention to who they are and what is important to them.

THE WOW EXPERIENCE FROM FEELING WANTED

Rosanna Durruthy is the head of Global Diversity, Inclusion, and Belonging at LinkedIn. Earlier I highlighted a few ways LinkedIn is working to operationalize belonging. It is a tricky endeavor. No one can make someone experience belonging. It cannot be manufactured through fun events, clever programs, or executive mandates. We each decide if our experience at work leads us to feel valued, wanted, and welcomed, but the experience can be intentionally set in motion. It takes coordination. It takes authenticity. It takes vulnerability.

Where LinkedIn has an edge over other large companies is in its commitment from leaders to inspiring belonging up and down the company hierarchy. Rosanna takes seriously her guardianship of a culture of belonging. For example, while most companies do an annual employee survey, LinkedIn employees provide feedback every six months. The DIBs team asks questions evaluating how much employees can be themselves at work, the quality of their work friendships, and if they feel that they belong in their team and at LinkedIn.[12] Each of these four inputs into the social media giant's equation are excellent starting points to measure and operationalize belonging.

While it is harder to measure how people feel, it is not impossible. Cadenced data collection linked to belonging helps leaders learn what does and does not work. An annual survey lumped into an employee engagement survey will not be sufficient for measuring belonging or other engagement topics. Additionally, pulse surveys, questions sent to employees on a daily or near daily basis, are too frequent.

The issue I have with pulse surveys is their often-haphazard strategy of determining what to measure. Question sets run the risk of asking unimportant questions or asking ones that cause unnecessary frustrations that the company is unprepared to handle. Additionally, daily or weekly pulse surveys collect an abundance of data that is hard to keep up with and analyze. Developing recommendations and circulating them among decision-makers for approval is also tricky. The risk of alienating employees with survey fatigue is high. Feedback loops that take months to release results often cause employees to doubt the top leaders' intent in asking for input.

In the timeworn employment paradigm (trade time for money), employees' skills are commodities. Managers look for people who closely match the skill sets needed. Once the ideal person is found, the trading begins. The employee works, applies skills, and receives a paycheck. Rinse. Repeat. Not only does this reinforce payment for skills it is also a slippery path to hiring someone to "fit in" the culture. Hiring for culture fit is a misinformed belief. Too much likeness among people reinforces conformity.

A more fruitful hiring practice is to bring someone into the company who compliments the culture. This shift also helps new employees see how they can contribute in a meaningful way. This benefits both the company and the employees. Think of complimentary hiring as part of human chemistry; you need many types of people to contribute their talents and strengths. This potent concoction of diversity leads to an alchemy that helps people see how to uniquely contribute their talents and strengths to the company's challenges. As Brené Brown's research on belonging has revealed, belonging has nothing to do with fitting in. It is about satisfying our craving as humans for connection.

A mindset shift to viewing employees as partners or collaborators is a beginning. From there, learning how to orchestrate bold, positive experiences at work is your next best step. Fortunately, this book can help you understand how to do that. One way to look at the ROI on belonging is to shorten the time to wow, a term championed by former Constant Contact CEO, Gail Goodman.[13]

> The time to wow is a nonlinear way to gauge how quickly employees' performance improves when they genuinely believe they are important to the company.

REDUCING THE TIME TO WOW VIA MEMORABLE MOMENTS

Authors Joseph Pine and James Gilmore lay out an invaluable framework, the 3-S Model, for creating memorable experiences.[14] While the framework was initially designed for customers, Pine and I both agreed it applies to the experience employees have at work.

A key point Pine and Gilmore make is that we have been conditioned to expect a mediocre experience—it is what most of us have known. It is also what we have been conditioned to accept as "that's the way it is." However, when applying the authors' model, new insights about how to shorten the time to wow emerge. The three inputs in Pine and Gilmore's model are increase satisfaction, decrease sacrifice, and increase surprise. For the model to work, all three must occur. Here is how Pine and Gilmore define the three inputs:

- Satisfaction: What is expected minus what is received
- Sacrifice: What is wanted minus what is settled for
- Surprise: What is perceived minus what is expected

A *satisfactory* work experience is what every employee wants. It "meets expectations," say Pine and Gilmore.[15] When I interviewed employees for my first book, *The Optimistic Workplace*, they told me that to have a positive work environment, essentials must be met: the right tools for the job, fair pay, and recognition for hard work, to name a few. The essentials from my research are conceptually similar to what Pine and Gilmore learned: if you want memorable moments, a satisfactory experience at work is table stakes. Bottom line: a satisfactory experience of belonging is the starting point for creating an experience of feeling wanted.[16]

If you recall from the previous chapter, positive and negative emotions shape how we experience anything, including work. The emotions are contagious. Now layer the influence of emotions on to employees having a satisfactory experience at work. If what they expect from their manager and the company and what they perceive to have received are not congruent, negative emotions surface. The contagion inherent in all emotions will either kill your efforts or positively accelerate them. The question is what could cause a satisfactory response to the experience of feeling wanted (or valued, for that matter)?

The second input in Pine and Gilmore's 3-S Model is *sacrifice*. If employees do not receive what they want from work (opportunities, flexibility, a sense of purpose), then they are settling for something that is suboptimal. Consider this example: An employee caring for an elderly parent wants a boss who understands the importance of family. However, her manager does not understand and is inflexible when her employee requests time off to take her dad to the doctor.

The employee must sacrifice her values to satisfy her boss's needs. Chronic sacrifice will generate hostility or even frustration (both negative emotions). The employee will share how she feels with others, and the contagion spreads. "To truly differentiate themselves, businesses must first focus on increasing satisfaction . . . then on eliminating . . . sacrifice, and [then] finally creating . . . surprise," say Pine and Gilmore.[17]

Creating a *surprising* experience at work does not necessarily entail planning elaborate events or offering expensive perks. A surprise could include a Bring Your Dog to Work policy. It could also be a monthly ask-the-CEO-anything-you-want event that is actually viewed as important. Both of these practices are uncommon, hence their surprising nature. Sure, some start-ups offer a wall of craft beer taps and cereal bars. Their novelty wears off, however. In a time when crappy workplace cultures are more common than great workplaces, it is not too difficult to surprise employees with a culture and climate that motivates and inspires great performances. Interactions and practices that are genuinely applied have a greater chance at shaping surprise than trendy, copy-and-paste cultural trends.

A logical question is, how do I use the 3-S Model as a leader? Fortunately, the companies we studied offer tangible inspirations. Check them out below. Identify which of the three inputs are embedded in each example.

- At Canlis Restaurant, the employees and the people leaders encourage and promote camaraderie on and off the clock. Sometimes the chef will make handmade pizzas and serve beer to employees after a night of delighting guests. Employees also spend time off the clock watching sports and getting to know one another.

Another example from Canlis is how employees are expected to surface ideas that align with the restaurant's purpose. For example, Maren Patrick, part of the management team, pitched an idea to use the rooftop bar for private cocktail receptions. The problem was that Canlis did not have a cocktail package for guests to purchase. Maren was immediately given the green light to develop the new offering. When was the last time you green-lighted a project without putting the employee through a bunch of bureaucratic hoops?

- At Barry-Wehmiller, employee Matt Gidley suggested that the company help rebuild a church in one of their remote locations. With community and family considered important to the company, CEO Bob Chapman approved the capital expenditures to rebuild the church.

The Barry-Wehmiller example wholly aligns with the company's values. Instead of fake proclamations that are common in corporate value statements, Chapman and his leadership team avoid patronizing platitudes that demotivate, infuriate, or chase away high performers. Instead, the leaders show employees how important the company values are by aligning their actions to those values. As for the other two examples, a frictionless road from idea to implementation also creates a positive experience. Leaders need to be conduits to progress. Old-school management beliefs are barriers to progress. Such beliefs hold that ideas must first be vetted by the employee's immediate manager. If the manager's ego is threatened by the idea or he just does not like it, the idea rarely moves up the hierarchy. This is a failure with significant repercussions. A great way to curtail innovative or controversial ideas is to demean employees by not unleashing their creativity, business savvy, and professional experiences.

The time to wow is not only applicable to new employees. Think of it as your way to monitor the time it takes new employees, disillusioned employees, or even high-performing employees to show they are committed to breakthrough performance. You can even look at it as a way to gauge how quickly the team pulls tighter together to deliver astonishing results. Think of time to wow as your barometer to belonging.

Historically speaking, human needs have been diminished in business. What makes us human has been disregarded in the pursuit of profit. After all, isn't it easier to not become emotionally invested in the people who actually do the hard work? This mindset has helped legacy companies across all industries and sectors create profitable cash cows.

But we have entered into a different time when companies are watched more closely and held to account for their actions. In truth, a company is nothing more than a legal designation and has no culpability on the effects it has on society, communities, and its employees. The people leading the company make the decisions and are responsible for the outcomes. Stepping out from behind the well-worn curtain that hid privileged executives from scrutiny is a new type of leader. These leaders see the duplicity in their role and welcome it.

That duplicity? It is (1) grow the business and (2) create the company's culture so that employees can create, innovate, plan, and implement solutions that are valued by customers. Equally as important is to honor and respect the sacrifices everyone makes so that the company thrives and remains relevant. Within this context, creating experiences that show employees they are valued, wanted, and welcomed is not a "nice to have." It is a differentiator.

CHAPTER 9

FEELING WELCOMED

The Generosity in a
Genuine Invitation

Our house was a place where you were welcome to make an idiot of yourself. Silliness was valued.

—Ty Burrel (American actor)

Why do vampires need to be welcomed into your home before entering it?

If you type this question in your favorite web browser, you will find hilarity, sincerity, and mockery.

My question has nothing to do with the protocols, history, or existence of vampires. It concerns the symbolism of an invitation.

When you are invited to a dinner party, it is an extension of the host's interest in who you are. The host wants to spend time with you. The host is interested in what you bring to the conversation at the dinner table. An invitation to someone's home is a grand gesture that says, "I trust you. I like you. Welcome."

Now, you may work with vampires. (Apparently it is not easy to spot them according to one discussion thread I read online.) But we'll leave vampire issues to their hunters. I want to draw your attention to the invitation you extend to your employees. What does your invitation—to work in your company or on your team—communicate? How do you show that every "type" of person is welcome in your company? Your team?

Unsatisfied with the web results to the question I posed at the opening of this chapter, I turned to social media, asking my family and friends. One response that stood out from the others came from Chad Balthrop, a pastor in Oklahoma. Chad and I have been online friends for a decade. Like most pastors I know, Chad is articulate and insightful about the nature of being human. Here's what Chad said: carefully consider the consequences involved when you welcome others into your home.[1]

Putting aside the evil symbolism of vampires, Chad's observation about who you invite into your home runs parallel to whom you bring into your company. I am a firm believer in hiring slowly. The invitation to join your company is one of the most important early gestures you extend as a leader. It is the start of an important relationship.

Feeling welcomed is the final experience that shapes belonging at work. It is first a reassurance that we are in the right place; we made the right choice to be part of this team.

Second, feeling welcomed is about psychological safety—a familiarity and level of comfort that encourages us to confidently share our ideas. Feeling safe in the right place is the equation for feeling welcomed.

PRIMAL HUMAN NEEDS ARE WORK NEEDS TOO

"If we're not being recognized by other humans, our stress levels go up, our productivity levels go down," says Paul Zak, who I quoted in chapter 2. I must confess that I have an intellectual crush on Paul Zak. His highly intricate research and his disarming way of talking about really nerdy, aka scientific, topics make him compelling. Zak studies the many implications oxytocin has on trustworthiness, economics, and the workplace.[2]

Authentic acknowledgment of others is not a perfunctory act. It is a genuine expression of interest in the other person. However, we all have feigned interest in others. We ask, "How was your weekend?" but have no true desire to hear the play-by-play of a colleague's highlight reel.

When our primal need to feel connected with others is satisfied, the connection helps us move past obligation and into feeling welcomed. As a leader, think of the passing casual conversations you have with employees. Zak recommends that when your and a colleague's paths cross, be inquisitive about what you observe: "You look happy today." Your specific observation signals that you pay attention to other people's body language and facial expressions. When you verbalize your observations, it opens a more meaningful interaction and signals that you paid attention to the other person. "You welcome [others] in an emotional way," says Zak.[3]

I've touched upon many human needs throughout this book: experiences of belonging, being loved, our survival instinct, and even being happy. These basic components of what it means to be human are what divides or unifies your work tribe. Their existence and influence in a work context are no different from when we spend time with friends or go out on a first date. So why do we ask our employees, even ourselves, to put them aside when we arrive at work? It is impossible for your amygdala to not go into protection mode when a colleague throws you under the bus. The unique opportunity you have as a people leader is to relate differently with your direct reports. You no longer need to separate being human with being at work. In fact, you need to be human to do great work. Anything short of that creates dysfunctions that limit your potential and your team's, too.

FRIENDS IN HIGH PLACES AND IN THE NEXT CUBICLE

In the last chapter I recounted Brent Stewart's story of feeling wanted. Brent is a newer manager and the cohost of the company's podcast, *Everybody Matters*. He is also a musician. As a creative, Brent is familiar with receiving feedback and input on his creations. In healthy organizations and high-performing teams, feedback is an essential ingredient to success.

Hearing the feedback, though, is not always easy. When we bring our work to colleagues and ask for input, our credibility is also subject to scrutiny. We are making ourselves vulnerable, an uncomfortable place for most, especially in a professional environment. "Will they think I don't know what I'm doing?" "I can't show weakness." "I don't want them to think I'm unprepared."

If Brent's boss made feedback personal, Brent would likely stop seeking feedback. He might conclude that he would never seek out his boss's approval and thus is not likely to hear praise for his hard work. The quality of the relationship would either be weak or, worse, destructive.

Does belonging change how we view approval and appreciation? Wrapped up in the knot of nervousness in our gut is the anticipation of hearing what others think of our work product. High-resonate relationships are a motivator for seeking feedback. They change the interaction between team members, and we learned from the model companies that resonate relationships are often friendships.

Friend or Acquaintance?

Brian and Mark Canlis place high importance on "being in relationship." When I pressed the brothers to give that phrase meaning in a business context, Mark immediately jumped in to clarify what to some people might sound like hippy-talk. He began by explaining that their restaurant's values are declarations of who all employees, including the brothers and their family members, want to become. "I think [that] trust is the currency of any relationship. I think that flourishing relationships do so in a place of generosity . . . generosity to me is not a financial word. It is a condition of the heart," Mark's thoughtful and reflective answer feels genuine. After all, this is the restaurant with a mission to turn people toward one another. What I found intriguing and even romantic is what he said next. "It is a condition of the heart or one's character such that I am willing to make space for you. If we are in relationship, I am a safe space for you." Mark concludes that being in relationship with one another boils down to three things: being trustworthy, safety, and others-centered. The last is a mindset reinforcing that the "world doesn't revolve around me."[4]

The intimacy that colors Mark's explanation of relationships is a meaningful way to distinguish friends from acquaintances. While some may believe friendships have no place at work, the Canlis family and research disagree. Gallup's engagement research finds that having a best friend at work leads to greater performance levels. Thirty-six percent fewer safety incidents. Seven percent greater customer engagement. Twelve percent higher profit.[5]

Friends are different from acquaintances. They have a closeness, a warmth, and a deeper level of respect. Social scientists explain acquaintances as weaker relationships where the history and familiarity with one another is limited and not as meaningful when compared to friendships. Friends show more empathy towards one another and are willing to understand differences. Acquaintances have not been through hell and back with you. They come and go based on need. As a leader, these distinctions may sound academic. However, what academics have found is also what Gallup's research finds: teams powered by friendships outperform teams that are predominately shaped by acquaintances.[6]

Let's Take That Hill Together

The experience of feeling welcomed is knowing that you *have* a place in the team. It is not about knowing *your* place in the team, however. The nuance is subtle but important. Think of having a place on the team like sitting down to a family dinner. There is always a table setting for you—or one will be made should you show up unexpectedly. Conversely, knowing your place on a team comes with conditions and rules. You need to follow them to stay in line with some social hierarchy. It is hard to experience the bonding elements of belonging when you have to abide by conditions and rules that you may not know about or agree with.

In the context of a work environment, people leaders are expected to achieve the goals assigned to them. Increasingly, companies are asking leaders to accomplish bigger, more daunting tasks and, oh by the way, you do not get more people or money. I have seen the destruction to team morale and results caused by the tension from "do more with less." Too often, though, leaders underestimate what a group of motivated and coordinated people can accomplish despite the metaphorical uphill climb.

Actually, researchers leveraged the metaphor of taking a hill together and designed an experiment around it. Using a steep hill as part of the challenge, they recruited pairs of friends to walk together and individuals to walk alone. Those who were alone were told to imagine being with an acquaintance. Everyone was taken to the bottom of a steep hill. Carrying backpacks filled with weights, both groups—the pairs of friends and the solo walkers—were asked to estimate the steepness of the hill. If you have ever visited San Francisco, imagine one of those steep hills and having to climb it with a weighted backpack.

The friends estimated the hill to be less steep than the individual who imagined climbing with an acquaintance. This experiment was not a physical test. Its purpose was to learn what motivational influences friends have on daunting tasks. What was the outcome? Researchers consistently learned that friendships contributed to motivational advantages, meaning the friends worked harder together. They communicated more effectively. Conflict was handled quickly, and the friends continually encouraged one another. In similar experiments, the absence of friendships led to social loafing, coasting on the hard work of others but doing little to help. Communications were also noted as inefficient.[7]

Friends tend to be tactfully candid with one another. When we talk with an acquaintance, uncertainty colors our interactions. What does it take to move from a casual relationship, with little-to-nothing emotionally invested in it, to a friendship? Experiencing feeling valued, wanted, and welcomed. The surprising secret to breakthrough performance, despite people and budget constraints, is the bonding influence of belonging.

We go the extra mile for our friends. Repeatedly we heard from employees at Canlis that they believed managers had their back. They believed that if they took a risk and it failed, that they would find support and not condemnation. It is far easier for resonate relationships to deepen when people feel safe.

Earlier in this chapter I wondered if belonging changes how we view approval and appreciation. Bruce and I did not set out to measure the influence that belonging has on seeking approval from colleagues or on shaping our view of appreciation. Anecdotally, I would say belonging turns appreciation into a language of gratitude. When a friend on a team tells you she appreciates your hard work or your stepping in and covering for her, the meaning and sentiment feels genuine. As for seeking approval, belonging does not eradicate this from our relationships. I've worked with high-performing teams that were competitive and had fun outdoing one another. I suspect there is a hint of approval-seeking in such instances. I suggest that the approval-seeking behavior has a healthier intent.

When fitting in shapes relationships, seeking the approval of the boss is often done to receive "favorite status" or to receive favorable treatment that ultimately reinforces fitting in. Approval and expressed appreciation are social behaviors. As a people leader, you want pro-social behaviors that deepen the bonds between teammates. Nobody has time to relive junior high school where kickball teams were formed based on popularity instead of talent.

Promoting friendships among teammates is perhaps the most appreciable act of leadership that you can take. This is not the only way to show employees that they have a place in your team. Instead of listing obvious tactics that promote feeling welcomed, I want to share the information that serves as an endless source of ideas. Think of it as the wellspring to feeling welcomed.

In his British accent, Lewis Garrad quickly gets to the heart of a significant influence on feeling welcomed. Garrad is an industrial and organizational psychologist I inter-viewed for this book. He succinctly tells me that a leader needs to understand who a person is to help him or her feel welcomed. Easier said than done, right? Garrad agrees. "While people are consistent and similar in many ways, it's actually their differences that provide the kind of color to social interactions."[8]

What Garrad is getting at is the riskiness inherent in oversimplifying a human need like belonging. His caution is worth heeding. As a leader, you are constantly evaluating individual needs and the needs of the group, and often the needs are at odds with each other. So, what are you to do? Feeling welcomed means one thing to one employee and something altogether different for another. Perhaps one of your employees really couldn't care less about having a seat at the table. What then?

The answer rests not just with you, but, ironically with the team too. Simply because you say there's a place for everyone at the table, it may not be modeled by the team. (Frankly, this is true for all three experiences of belonging.) The wellspring I referenced earlier holds an answer to spreading the love inherent in feeling welcomed. The answer is found in gratitude.

Before you roll your eyes and groan, I want to give you a peek at the human needs that make gratitude invaluable. Its effects are best realized when it is contagious.

186

Most of us, hopefully, were raised to say thank you when someone helps us or does something nice for us. The phrase "thank you" has become so overused that it has lost its significance. However, unsuspecting minds may not realize how influential expressions of gratitude are to our sense of competence and to feeling connected to others. In short, our social worth is wrapped up in feeling valued and welcomed.

Research from Adam Grant, mentioned in chapter 3, and Francesca Gino, professor at University of North Carolina at Chapel Hill, finds that communal expressions of gratitude are more impactful than individual contributions.

Communal expressions of gratitude contribute to our feeling worthy because our efforts impact other people's lives. Conversely, when our own efforts receive praise, it reinforces our sense of competence. Both are important, but helping other people is considered more meaningful to us.[9]

The benefits of belonging are realized when the entire team experiences them, not just one or two people. To help spread the experience of feeling welcome, Grant's and Gino's findings point to a shared cultural practice: "Gratitude expressions provide concrete evidence that [team members'] actions matter in the lives of beneficiaries."[10] Your team needs to communicate that they value one another's help. This task cannot rest on your shoulders alone. It is a team responsibility, not just a leader's.

You don't need to convene a project team to plan ways to express gratitude. Revisit what we were taught in grade school and apply it to your adult relationships: Help your colleagues. Thank them for their support. Consider what Grant and Gino add to the timeless lesson; extend your perspective beyond the personal satisfaction that comes from helping others. A practice of gratitude encourages each person on the team to want to continue to help. When we feel valued for our contribution and are thanked for it, the welcome mat is always there. There is no need for an invitation. Come in. Sit at the table, and join the conversation.

As I wrote this chapter's concluding thoughts, I began to worry how basic this final message sounds. "Am I insulting my readers' intelligence?" But helping people feel welcomed is not complicated. In this politically and socially divisive time, a simple, straightforward solution could be helpful. Nevertheless, I am aware that saying thank you to show teammates that they are welcomed may be an oversimplification.

I will end this chapter with a nudge. It is not the act of saying thank you that matters. It is how a genuine thank you lets the other person know that you are paying attention. That you, despite your crazy schedule, value showing to your colleagues that their support matters.

Be genuine when being grateful.

Be specific when expressing gratitude.

And say thank you in person instead of in an email or a text message.

CHAPTER 10

WHEN COMPANIES CARE

Ending the Practice of Pretending

As we look ahead into the next century, leaders will be those who empower others.

—Bill Gates

Sometimes you need to stand alone to know you belong. Hamdi Ulukaya, founder and CEO of Chobani, decided to give jobs to European refugees at the same time Donald Trump was elected as president of the United States. With promises of a wall to keep out illegal immigrants, Trump's "America First" rhetoric made Ulukaya's decision controversial. In an interview with a *Fast Company* journalist, Ulukaya, an immigrant himself, detailed the somewhat violent pushback and resistance he had received. From boycotts of Chobani's Greek yogurt products, to death threats, to online attacks, Ulukaya's choice to show compassion to the refugees was un-American.

When the *New York Times* learned of the threats, the newspaper published a story revealing Ulukaya's intentions to help refugees make a life for themselves and position them to contribute to society. The Turkish CEO's principles may have initially made him feel alone, but he quickly learned that he was not. After the story ran, hundreds of letters of support for Ulukaya's leadership decision showed that he had his own tribe of supporters.[1]

In 2017, Chobani booked nearly $2 billion in sales[2] and had 54 percent of the Greek yogurt market share.[3] Chobani is number one in its market category. While that is certainly impressive, without employees' enthusiastic support and commitment, this rapid growth would not have been possible. Certified as a Great Place to Work company, 89 percent of employees feel welcome and 90 percent are proud to tell others that they work for Chobani. Overall, 83 percent of employees say Chobani is a great place to spend most of their waking hours.[4]

From what I've read about Hamdi Ulukaya, he is unyielding in his fight for the greater good. His beliefs have caused trouble for him, yet he continues to stand up for them. Now more than two thousand employees stand with their esteemed leader, proudly showing their support for a man who built a company that cares about them.

Up to this point in the book I've focused predominately on your role in shaping belonging. The company also plays a part. In fact, an argument could be made that without support at a company level, belonging will be slow to transform teams, people, and results. While I do not fully believe that belonging cannot be realized without company support, there is no viable argument that belonging can be achieved without some level of company infrastructure to support it. Fortunately, companies like Chobani are models to study. So are the model companies we studied. What follows is the breakdown of what we learned from them.

IT'S LIKE WHEN PEANUT BUTTER AND CHOCOLATE COME TOGETHER

Today, a business wields incredible influence on communities, employees, and even social and political discourse. That influence can be used for ill or goodwill. Naturally, how you or I classify *ill* or *goodwill* is subjective. Yet the widening gap between our willingness to understand and learn from our differences and channel them in a constructive way is eroding civility.

Business leaders have an opportunity to signal to employees that collaboration, curiosity, and compassion are nonnegotiable tenants of achieving the extraordinary. When we as a society and you as a leader hesitate or rationalize behaviors that undermine the safety, the joy, or whatever gets people up in the morning and wanting to be at your workplace, then intolerance prevails. When intolerance prevails, and there will always be intolerance of differences, your work as a leader is harder. Yes, we do bandy the term *leadership* back and forth to the point it loses its meaningful potency. However, a hackneyed term does not mean its relevance is lessened.

The honor in becoming a manager is still a career milestone. But the honor in helping others find fulfillment in their work or learn about themselves in surprising ways—these are what leaders cause. The mindset. The heart. The patience. I could go on and on, but these are what is transformed in the leader. The satisfaction and happiness far exceed a career milestone. It becomes a meaningful moment of your own.

A great pairing, like peanut butter and chocolate or Starsky and Hutch, is compelling. So is a leader who has found his or her place in a company. Truly great leadership within a supportive environment is a winning combination.

What, however, does a company need to establish for the leaders to influence belonging within their teams? Themes from our interview data pointed to *expectations*. It wasn't as if everyone in our model companies was having conversations about belonging. Belonging was an outcome from practicing it values, like at LinkedIn. Or because of the tone set by the owners, like at Canlis. Or because of the belief in human potential, like at Barry-Wehmiller.

By their own style, each company had their version of expectations. We identified six expectations that we named tribal knowledge. From here through the end of the book, I'll use expectations and tribal knowledge interchangeably. The part to remember with each of the examples is they are expectations your company has of you and your team.

TRIBAL KNOWLEDGE

It is important to note that the tribal knowledge is not for managers only. The knowledge is shared up and down the company. Some of the tribal knowledge is more suited to individuals or teams or both. Figure 10.1 is an overview of the categories of tribal knowledge. Let's look at each one. I give you some examples too.

FIGURE 10.1

Tribal Knowledge Shaping the Experience of Belonging at Work		
Tribal Knowledge	**Who**	**Belonging Practices**
Prioritize Purpose	Individual and Team	A focus on serving and working with colleagues; clear intent to make a difference for stakeholders; a shared identity of the colleague community; value work/ life harmony to provide vitality and energy when at work
Ambition	Individual	Clarity of performance expectations; frequent reviews of performance results; team health is prioritized as paramount to performance; bone deep pride for and because of the work; a focus on what's possible; rewarding work and being rewarded for doing great work; promote creativity and freedom of thought
Adaptive Awareness	Leader	Be consistent and knowable; socialize and discuss the mission and vision in interactions (micro interactions and gatherings); uses the Leadership Code. See Figure 11.1.
Commitment	Individual and Team	Trust and be trustworthy; consistently show you have each other's back; practice spontaneous generosity; demonstrate you care about people beyond their role and accomplishments; demonstrate who you are and what you value; play together as a team
Curiosity	Individual	Quickly initiate difficult conversations (Connect to be direct); show others that they are heard; offer balanced feedback; tap into your intuition when exploring differences; develop a practice of transparent communications; promote psychological safety (Candid Advantage)
Team Practice	Individual and Team	Learn together; generate enthusiasm through work that energizes; constantly seek out and explore growth opportunities

Prioritize Purpose

The hospitality industry does an extraordinary job in creating memorable experiences. A great customer experience thrives when the employee experience inspires and motivates. Among the model companies we studied, Canlis stands out with how purpose is prioritized. I heard Brian and Mark in separate conversations weave in the restaurant's purpose when talking with team members. Oftentimes it was a brief part of the interaction. It never came across as a sales pitch or was delivered like forced compliance. It also shapes the fun they have. During the team dinner, a colleague will go to the front of the room and do an adult version of show-and-tell. On the day we were at the restaurant, a new employee was at the head of the room. He was funny. Charming. With encouragement and laughter from his new colleagues, it was over in about two minutes. We heard stories about shares that brought people to tears. There were personal shares and even lessons in life.

At Canlis, prioritizing purpose is best understood in action. The show-and-tell is an extension of the restaurant's mission: turn people to one another. The surest way to get people to connect is through stories, emotions, and a dash or two of vulnerability. Another way purpose is prioritized is by designing a reservation process around the importance of relationships. Management meetings are structured to ensure everyone is on the same page. They are efficient in that everyone comes prepared, so they can help get the restaurant ready for the first seating.

While Canlis is the smallest-sized company that we studied, their commitment to the restaurant's purpose undoubtedly helped them consistently delight guests. A restaurant does not easily earn a Michelin star. To earn one, two, or three stars is a proud accomplishment. When Gordon Ramsay, the TV celebrity chef, lost a star from his restaurant in New York, he compared it to the loss of a girlfriend.

Purpose, when it is prioritized as the company's North Star, not only shapes how people perform at work but also encourages them to prioritize their own purpose awareness. In one study, 39 percent of employees with a strong sense of purpose were likely to stay another three or more years with their present company. Seventy-three percent were satisfied with their job. In the same study, companies known to have a strong purpose had a higher number of page views and online interactions on their LinkedIn page.[5]

Ambition

In every company's burn pile should be its annual performance review process. You know the ones: where once every twelve months (and that may be generous) a manager sits down with employees. In the awkward exchange, the manager discusses/reads her employee's wins and "next times." The same wins and mess-ups that are written by the employee for his manager. The successes are written a bit more robustly with a dose of forced humility or awkward boasting. The "next times" or "learning moments" are carefully worded to not cause undue influence on the meager 2 percent pay increase awaiting the employee once the agony of the ritual is over.

Of course, today the pendulum has swung in the other direction. Employees are asked daily how they feel, what is their mood, what do they hope to accomplish this year, and on and on and on. This practice generates too much feedback, rendering it meaningless to forgetful.

In the teams we interviewed, achievement was shaped by more meaningful influences on behavior and performance. But money is still important to inspiring performance. Kip Tindell said this about paying employees: "I always say the hardest thing you can train managers to do is to pay people well. They think somehow that they need to protect the company by paying people poorly. What that does is hurt the company." The philosophy is straightforward: Hire people with strong ambition. If managers want top talent but won't pay for it, then the company is limiting its best effort to succeed.[6]

We know, however, that money's influence on ambition wears thin quickly. What we learned from The Container Store and the other model companies is that traditional carrots, like more money or feedback, are still useful. But these companies go further to fire up their employees. From employees at Barry-Wehmiller, we repeatedly heard examples of how the company's human-centered culture is a source of pride: A new employee astonished that Barry-Wehmiller would fly in family members to celebrate an employee's success; a young superstar with doubt about her future is mentored by a senior leader and later becomes an executive herself. In each of the stories, pride fueled employees' ambition. When people feel valued, wanted, and welcomed, they want to give back to the company. At Canlis, servers constantly study the restaurant's secret playbook to become masters at contributing to each guest's dining experience. That experience, by the way, begins even before they arrive at the restaurant.

Admittedly, when something is not working my first inclination is to start over and make what's broken better. As the idiom goes, "Don't throw out the baby with the bath water." Breathe new life into old practices that better inspire your team. Simplify your pay-for-performance expectations. Rollout a team performance bonus plan and related goals. Play together as a team. These are all ways to spike ambition. They all have one thing in common—appealing to basic human needs of connection, hard work, safety, and, oh, belonging.

Adaptive Awareness

Of all the tribal knowledge categories, adaptive awareness is arguably the most difficult one to practice. If you recall from part 1, I used the Rolling Stones as an example of a team with great chemistry. The hidden currents between Jagger and Richards have contributed to some of rock's greatest songs and onstage performances. When the two musicians perform together, they rely on cues between them to signal the direction they want to go.

The ability to read your teammates and pivot without saying something is adaptive awareness. There are only a few ways to achieve this level of connection and communication. One is that it takes practice: failing together, learning together, even having fun together. Another way is to spend time with colleagues outside of work. Our lives are shaped by a collection of stories and life experiences. Not all stories can be told or understood when at the office.

Adaptive awareness is not something you'll see a company list as an expectation, unless of course it is the military. In non-military environments, teams with this heightened communication skill not only spend time together outside of work but each person on the team also invests considerable time raising their own self-awareness.

When I work with leaders, we inevitably talk about being consistent and knowable. This is how you help your team learn your idiosyncrasies and how you respond to situations. You can have bad days. You can have a mood swing from angry to delightful within ten minutes. How you handle situations needs to be consistent. The more your team learns how you respond to a variety of situations, the more knowable you become.

Adaptive awareness may be the most difficult category for teams to develop, because it requires both you and your team to learn to read subtle behavioral cues. You must be vulnerable and allow others to see you raggedy and even unpolished. Adaptive awareness also needs trust. It takes time for a team to develop this strong intuitive interaction. The good news is that when there is a strong sense of belonging, adaptive awareness is a bit easier to achieve.

Commitment

Historically, companies have asked employees for their loyalty. Loyalty originally meant committing years to a company. In return, the company would reward you with a great promotion and pension. Don't confuse commitment for loyalty. In the companies we studied, commitment was not to one's self or work, but to the team.

The subtle shift of focus away from self onto the team is a powerful enabler of belonging. In Figure 10.1, notice how the practices listed improve the performance of the team. For belonging to occur, assuming positive intent significantly influences commitment.

When you assume positive intent, it is easier to trust and be trustworthy. Likewise, when a teammate does not deliver the best performance, that person isn't thrown under the bus. The whole team backs up their colleague and helps him grow from the experience. As commitment to the team's success yields more wins, spontaneous generosity—expressions of gratitude, different ways to say thank you—turns into a fun way of celebrating together.

The tribal knowledge within Canlis expects employees to address concerns with a colleague directly. The logic is quite simple. If a person is worried about a teammate, ignoring the signs or delaying a candid conversation will eventually impact the team's performance.

Commitment is a fundamental principle that influences the experience of belonging. It establishes a shared understanding that the team wins or fails together. Therefore, a premium is placed on team practice that facilitates winning, for example preparing together for major presentations or job shadowing to deepen the team's bench strength.

Commitment to team success helps Olympic champions win gold. At the 2008 Beijing Olympics, the British cycling team won 70 percent of the available gold medals in track cycling. Prior to this, Britain's cycling team had won gold only once in its seventy-six-year history. The tipping point for the team's dramatic pivot was due to *marginal gains.*

Marginal gains is making a series of small changes that accumulate into major improvements. For example, Sir David Brailsford, who coached the Brits to their gold glory, and the team made microadjustments to make the bikes more aerodynamic. They painted the floor white in the team trucks to better spot any dust, which undermines bike maintenance. A team doctor taught proper hygiene to keep the team well. The team also did not shake hands at the Winter Olympics to avoid germs. All of these minor tweaks made in succession amounted to a competitive advantage that yielded tremendous success.[7]

For marginal gains to be effective, a team's mindset needs to shift from individual performance to individual and group performance. Look for ways to remove barriers, watch for friction points that slow momentum, identify extraneous policies that limit a team's ability to achieve big wins. Institute practices that develop team members' reliance on one another.

A team that can move together in a coordinated manner relies on a strong practice of commitment: commitment to the team's performance and to bringing your best effort to your assignments.

Curiosity

By now it should be clear that each tribal knowledge expectation is not basic or simple. On the surface they seem routine. In practice they require you to split your focus. You need to be willing to navigate your contribution to the team's performance while also helping the team perform together. This duality will cause team members to collide, metaphorically speaking. Conflict will arise. Tempers will flare. Disagreements will surface. Good. Good. And good. Teams that tap into the cohesive value of belonging will get testy with each other. It's how the collisions are handled that distinguishes teams with high belonging from teams without it.

In tense moments, curiosity helps ease tensions. In fun times, curiosity adds levity and playfulness. When times are tense, a practice of candid conversations helps to quickly resolve differences. We labeled the expectation that companies have of quickly resolving differences: *candid advantage.*[8]

Candid advantage is a practice of initiating potentially difficult conversations within a few hours of the breakdown. The skill required to practice this is what we call "connect to be direct." In other words, before you blast your colleague with all the reasons you are upset, you initiate the conversation by giving some context then move into the candid, and always respectful, feedback. Here are examples:

- "Brady, while you were traveling on business, a few unexpected events were scheduled. I did not have time to update you while you were on the road. Unfortunately, this meant you did not have all the details you like to have for our meetings this morning. I know you don't like to be surprised with last-minute details, but taking your frustrations out on the team is also not helpful. Let's go over what you need so you feel up to speed."

- "Kip, in our stand-up meeting this morning, did you notice how your wake upset some of the people on our team? We all understand the pressure that you're under. At the same time, we are here to help you. It's hard to do that when your actions push us away. What do you need to help you ease your stress levels?"

When I coach managers who struggle with conflict, I share this quote: "Be curious, not confrontational." Nobody likes to be confronted. It elevates our fight-or-flight response. Words are said that cannot be unsaid. Not much good will come from our lizard brain's response when we think we're under attack. Instead, use curiosity to explore behaviors that undermine performance.

Here the expectation from the company is clear: When you make a mess, clean it up, and everyone moves on. There is no need to hang on to hurt feelings when we call out each other on behaviors that threaten team performance.

Team Practice

Of all the expectations in this list of tribal knowledge, team practice was a surprise. If you have ever played sports, you immediately get the importance of team practice. In baseball, teams practice drill after drill after drill: fielding ground hits, sliding, running, reading hand signals. In companies, it is rare for teams to practice their craft together. A bunch of individuals are cobbled together, applying their professional skills to complete their assignments.

Belonging changes the dynamics by reinforcing interdependency. A great example is the executive team's meeting at Canlis. Each night before the team dinner, the executives ensure they all know every reservation for the night, any special requests, how to handle less-common requests (like getting a ninety-year-old man up a flight of stairs because the restaurant doesn't have an elevator), sharing information that will help the hostesses delight guests. They practice this drill six days a week.

The goal of team practice in a business setting is simple: build familiarity with how the team interacts together. In sports, practice builds muscle memory. Muscle memory establishes a familiarity with doing things "right," so you know when something is "wrong." In business, familiarity is knowing where the handoffs are and to whom. It's knowing the strengths and weaknesses of your teammates and adjusting on the fly. It can also be learning or prioritizing workload together. Team practice requires everyone to know everyone else's swim lane, or area of expertise. This makes it easier to ask for help or to switch swim lanes, even temporarily. Team practice also builds comfort in relying on others to help chop the wood and carry the water—doing the routine work that nobody really enjoys but that must be done in the spirit of progress: sharing responsibility for leading meetings, showing up prepared to meetings, pinch-hitting for a colleague when he is out sick.

Teams that practice together move swiftly together.

Teams that move swiftly together enjoy working together. They also celebrate together. The dynamics are organic, not mechanical. The close friendships come from a sense of belonging. That sense of belonging deepens as the relationships deepen. In time, the experience of belonging makes it easier for teams to align with and mature their tribal knowledge.

It may occur to some of you that I'm reinforcing the time required to understand tribal knowledge. Employees today work for a company for about three years and then move on. Fortunately, the benefits from the tribal knowledge can be realized in short time frames. What helps facilitate their benefits is immediate immersion in the company's culture. From day one leaders need to show how central the six expectations are to how the company runs. What's more, incorporate the tribal knowledge into your hiring process. Screen for a person's ability to depend on others for success. Run scenarios assessing a candidate's tolerance for bravely engaging in conflict. Look for instances of vulnerability and ask the candidate to articulate how he or she felt in the moment.

Finally, for teams already in place, leverage the science of experiences. Teams that go through a struggle or challenge are primed to develop deeper bonds. What external influence can you inject into your team's dynamics that will bring them together and help them learn how to overcome a challenge? I'm not talking about trust falls or ropes courses. Those are fun but do not build the interdependency we just explored. Instead, give them a project important to the department or the company. Coach them on ways to apply the tribal knowledge to their processes. And let them fail. Then help them recover if they are unsure how.

When your company sets the tone that they care about employees—their performance, their well-being, their success, their humanity—it helps you as the people leader to up your game. The final chapter will detail what it can look like using belonging to unify your work tribe.

CHAPTER II

CAPTAINS OF CONTEXT

The Honor in Uniting
and Connecting

O Captain! My Captain! Our fearful trip is done,
The ship has weather'd every rack, the prize we sought is won.
                                                    —Walt Whitman

A ffairs of the heart can be confusing. Inspiring. Capti-
vating. The honor in leading people is an affair of the
heart. It is what makes leading people the greatest challenge in your career. The storms that beat up the symbolic boat
in Walt Whitman's poem are the storms that challenge you and
your team in its journey. Upon the boat's return to the shore,
the captain in Whitman's poem is discovered dead. Albeit a
bit dramatic—poetically and in my comparison here—the

message is an important one. Yes, leading people to work together will test your patience. The wins and losses and the valleys and peaks challenge your resolve. Through it all, you need to return from your journeys as a leader intact, fulfilled, and ready to go out on another journey. It is what we do.

I worry about the well-being of the leaders I meet. They carry the entire burden of their crew on their shoulders and in their hearts, and they ruminate on the issues preventing them from sleeping. Poor health and well-being is often an issue for the leaders I meet. But, despite their weathered bodies and every rack that bruises their efforts, the best leaders get back on the "ship" and go after the "prize," knowing the unknown will threaten to throw the team off course.

I firmly believe, especially after visiting the model companies and hearing their employees' stories, that belonging is an invaluable experience that will help leaders and teams to triumph over the corporate storms.

In this final chapter, you will learn what you can do to contribute to the experiences of belonging. Yes, I have shared many examples of what other companies are doing. I have saved the best for last, though. In our review of the interview data, Bruce and I codified the leadership actions from the model companies. Figure 11.1 gives you a very high-level overview of what we call the leadership code.

The leadership code is what you can lean on to shape the context, or the work environment, to bring belonging to your team or tribe. The leadership code helps unite your team and connect them to learn in new ways. It helps you teach your team how important they are to each other's success.

Belonging is tribal. As such, it takes the entire tribe to nurture the experiences from feeling valued, wanted, and welcomed.

FIGURE 11.1

Leadership Code		Definition
	Be Grounded in Business Fundamentals	The thin line between success and excess
	Continuously Elevate Excellence	The team that trains together moves faster together
	Do It for the Tribe	The team's health is paramount
	Know Your Position's Province	Own the reality that your role has an impact
	Grow Your Leadership Vitae	Your success is determined by what you leave behind
	Know Your Center of Gravity	Lead from values and attitudes that promote team and individual success

THE LEADERSHIP CODE

In 2018, I made my first trip to Hawaii. I was inspired by the Hawaiians' respect for their history, preserving their culture and dealing with the threats to their heritage. I mean no disrespect when I say this: there are strong parallels between Hawaiian culture and company culture.

As a leader, you have been tasked to help your company remain relevant. As times change, attitudes evolve, and new ways of running a business push your company, your culture and history can get lost amid the chaos. Hawaiians have a value that is a powerful influence on navigating the chaos, and it can help you remain focused on belonging and keeping your team together. The term is *lōkahi*.

> *Lōkahi* means harmony and unity. It requires coop-
> eration and collaboration to achieve great outcomes.

Think of *lōkahi* as a compass for your work as a captain of context. Context is merely the environment you help create. As the captain, your leadership presence is the greatest influence on the context and the experience of belonging. Since the goal is to create belonging, then harmony and unity are essential. How you maximize harmony and unity will help you facilitate the experiences linked to feeling valued, wanted, and welcomed.

The leadership code consists of six beliefs. As Bruce and I analyzed the interview data and transcripts, we pulled out every leadership example that contributed to employees' sense of belonging. We then grouped the leadership actions together. Table 11.1 shows the outcome of our analysis. What the table does not show you are full descriptions for each code. The descriptions are more detailed insights from the data. Table 11.1 gives you more context for each code.

TABLE II.I: LEADERSHIP CODE DESCRIPTIONS

Leadership Code	Leadership Coder Descriptions
Be Grounded in Business Fundamentals	The thin line between success and excess Belonging is a powerful human need. In a business environment, shaping belonging needs to be grounded in business results. When people work in an environment that fosters high performance and leaders show a genuine interest in the person it then becomes easier to accept responsibility for the outcomes of good work or mistakes. A supportive environment reduces the frustrations from high expectations and a toxic environment.
Continuously Elevate Excellence	The team that practices together moves faster together This ties directly to commitment as part of the tribal knowledge that shapes expectations for high performance.
Do It for the Tribe	The team's health is paramount Decisions need to evaluate how the tribe would be impacted when evaluating assignments, developing relationships, new hires, or anything that can enhance or reduce the experiences of feeling valued, wanted, or welcomed. When an outside influence threatens the cohesion of the tribe, there is a record of tribal consideration that helps the team bounce forward quickly from a setback.

Know Your Position's Province	Own the reality that your role has an impact
	Province means to maintain the proper focus, be aware of the influence that your activities have on others. Clarity in your province means clarity for your team. Out-of-scope requests are better managed when you know your province and the impact your wake has on others.
Grow Your Leadership Vitae	Your success is determined by what you leave behind
	A vitae is a historical sketch of your accomplishments. Any great vitae reflects the outcomes you helped influence. Continue to hone your leadership craft and let your results speak about your legacy
Know Your Center of Gravity	Lead from your values and attitudes that promote team and individual success
	In times when chaos forces you to lose your footing, modus vivendi* helps you back to your center of gravity, a place where you can lead with confidence.
	*Modus vivendi (or a manner of living that reflects your values and attitudes)

BELONGING BRINGS TOGETHER
BUSINESS RESULTS AND EXCELLENCE

For nearly three decades I have worked in various HR roles: learning and development, organizational behavior, organizational development, and change leader. I have become accustomed to being challenged about the value my roles bring to a company. So, I have made it a personal mission to always align the work we do with tangible results.

I was pleased to see time and again, employees and managers had developed practices that help them run the business and also inspire people to excel in their roles. What we saw in the model companies, though, was an intentional set of practices that helped employees understand the impact their work has on the business.

The Container Store trains its employees to understand how their behavior influences shoppers' buying decisions. Instead of taking a hard-sales approach, employees ask customers questions to understand the nature of their home project. It is a relational sales approach. This approach works best when employees understand the practical and the relational reasons for the sales philosophy. At LinkedIn, the DIBs team measures the impact their programs have on key metrics. This helps the team move past proving their value to executives and on to partnering with them to grow the business and evolve the culture.

If you model what you want from others, then it is easier to ask for it in return. When it comes to "Continuously Elevate Excellence" as a leader, your role is to bring your best self to work every day. It doesn't mean your best self will shine through all the time. Here are some of the examples we heard in our interviews:

- As a team, keep alive the conversation of what great leadership looks like. Discuss failures of leadership and the lessons learned. Spot examples of leadership that evoke positive responses. These conversations happen casually between employees and more intentionally in meetings.
- Always seek out ways to improve what you contribute to the team. Emulate through your own style your leaders' energy and enthusiasm. It's a clear signal of what your boss prefers, and it creates consistency for your team. If your boss does not exude energy and enthusiasm, it is all the more important for you to show it to your team.

DO IT FOR THE TRIBE

In previous chapters I wrote about the importance of resonate relationships. The leadership code "Do It for the Tribe" implies that a relational approach with employees will help inspire excellence. Here are themes for this code, which employees shared in our interviews:

- Know the demands of leadership: If you want to move into a formal leadership role, then accept the responsibilities of helping people succeed.

Leadership is about people. You need to like people and be curious to learn about them if you want to lead them.

- Be a relatable leader: What was fun to observe in the model companies was the great deal of camaraderie between employees and their bosses. CEOs were teased about their eating habits. New employees challenged their boss without hesitation. The relatable leader builds resonate relationships. These leaders openly shared their quirks, even made fun of them. They revealed personal information, making them human.

- "My role as a leader is to coordinate and enable the success of our community . . . I know I am a valuable and contributing member of the group." This was a direct quote from one of the managers at Barry-Wehmiller. Notice the parity to employees. This leader did not let the hierarchy dictate how she related to her team. While she clearly owns the responsibility for the team's results, she interacted with her team as colleagues.

- Have your team's back even if you think they are going down the wrong path. One of my mentors has a philosophy he calls "Fail fast, and don't worry about the mistake as long as it costs me less than $500,000." While your loss threshold may be lower, the message is clear—when we are working to change our customers' world, mistakes will be made. A hovering leader is a smothering leader. It is not helpful to the tribe's growth when a leader prevents teams from failing.

KNOW YOUR POSITION'S PROVINCE

Let's pause for a moment. Up to this point, the leadership code focused on you helping your team. The remaining three codes shift their focus. Instead of leading for the benefit of your team, "Know Your Position's Province" and the two codes that follow shift the focus inward.

While the inward focus helps you gain clarity and awareness of your impact, ultimately your team benefits. This distinction carries more importance today than ever before. As machine learning, artificial intelligence, and automation continue to do the routine, boring work humans used to do, companies are redirecting the workforce in new ways. Instead of firing employees because of the machines, companies are tasking humans to work together on more complicated problems. The conundrum, however, is that historically companies have invested more money in developing their workforce's technical and professional skills. Soft-skills training has received less attention but is needed for the evolving nature of work. Researchers are concerned that we are underskilled in this area, causing a gap in the workforce.

Self-awareness and self-reflection are two soft skills that are central to personal growth. The focus of "Know Your Position's Province" is knowing how your leadership impacts others. Recall Kip Tindell's analogy, "What's the wake you make?" If the wake you make is due to actions that are outside of your sphere, meaning not your responsibility, the wake you cause wreaks havoc on others. The leaders we observed and learned about kept their eyes on the activities entrusted to them for belonging to emerge and be sustainable. They could go wide and deep because they maintained a disciplined focus on their team's purpose. Here are some nuggets of wisdom they shared with Bruce and me:

- Know the impact of your wake on others.
- Embrace the philosophy that a leader is a steward: This simply means leadership is an act of service. Stewards operate from one simple question: "How can I help you?"
- Shift the problem's focus. In the early days of Barry-Wehmiller's culture transformation, the executive leadership team reframed problems by looking at the impact on employees.

Rhonda Spencer shared this example about the rising cost of worker's compensation. Using one of the company's leadership principles to reframe the issue—"We measure the success by the way we touch the lives of people"—the team realized the problem was not a worker's compensation problem. Rhonda said, "People that we care about are getting hurt in our plants. So let's solve the problem from that context."

Not only does Rhonda's example model a leadership principle important at Barry-Wehmiller, they responded in a way that made employees feel valued. A cross-functional team came together and reframed the problem into a statement about a desirable outcome: everyone has an equal right to and the responsibility for safety. Rhonda could have solved the problem, but she had the self-awareness to see that ownership of the solution rested with employees in the plant. The discussion the cross-functional team had ultimately led to an important distinction that influenced the rising workers' comp costs: is it better to finish something on time or to be safe? With the problem resolved by employees, Barry-Wehmiller costs dropped in half during the first year the new mindset was communicated.[1]

In our need to just get something done, even with a heroic mindset, we think it is faster to solve our employees' problems but we create problems for ourselves later. A codependent dynamic develops that teaches employees that they need us to solve their problems. That not only takes up more of your time but it also reduces the experience of feeling valued.

GROW YOUR LEADERSHIP VITAE AND KNOW YOUR CENTER OF GRAVITY

At the risk of sounding redundant, "Grow Your Leadership Vitae" is code for keep growing as a person, as a leader, and as a professional. What do you want to be known for when you leave your current position? A vitae is a historical document that summarizes your successes. Your success is determined by what you leave behind. Wise leaders will leave with things better than they found them. Know-it-all leaders leave behind expressions of gratitude that they are no longer there.

What helps you know that what you leave behind is *modus vivendi,* or living in a manner that aligns with your values and beliefs? Employees' enthusiasm in their stories for this code were both positive and cautionary. In the context of their current employer, they often made comparisons between the leaders at the model company and "bad" leaders at former employers. When Bruce and I examined the data for "Know Your Center of Gravity," Bruce compared this code to a boat.

A boat's center of gravity is influenced by weight. If the weight is evenly distributed, it will help the boat maximize its speed, economizing fuel and overall performance. If the center of gravity is off, then the speed, economies of scale, and performance are suboptimized.

Your center of gravity helps you lead your team via your leadership philosophy, your personal values, and even the team's purpose. When you lead from these three influences, your team can move more quickly and accomplish more. You need to know how to distribute your center of gravity in a way that helps you succeed in your work and support your team in their goals. Here are a few quotes that really drive home the point of knowing your center of gravity:

- "Employees suffer under poor leadership."
- "Absence of leadership puts teams in performance drift."
- "We're trying to get the better of each other and not where we are exchanging our time and energy for [money]."
- "Leadership success is defined by the success of the group and not the success of the individual in charge."[2]

Someone long ago said leadership is a contact sport. The game you are playing cannot be won behind a desk or from the sidelines. Wishing you had more authority, money, time, or people will not lead to winning the game. Nobody will be coming along to tap any of us on the shoulder and give us permission to create extraordinary experiences of belonging. The waiting period has ended. Now is your time to not only help your employees rediscover the joy in their work, but for you to discover it as well.

ON BELONGING

Canlis Restaurant was the first company Bruce and I studied. We arrived at the restaurant about fifteen minutes early. Lake Washington was calm as the summer sun began to send Seattle its warm wake-up call. It was quiet in the parking lot. We were unsure if we should walk into the restaurant or wait outside. I'm not sure why we hesitated. I suppose it was out of respect. After all, we hadn't meet anyone in person yet.

Katie Coffman was the first to arrive. She greeted us in a cheery mood. "You know, you could have just gone into the restaurant." Yeah, we know. It is only now, as I reflect over the start of our data collection, that I see the symbolism in our hesitation.

There is nothing more assuring than a warm welcome. Katie's smile, rapid-paced walk, and friendly demeanor perked me up. She welcomed us into the restaurant as she opened the unlocked door. Like a good host would do, she immediately explained the layout of the restaurant. Keep in mind she had just arrived at work and did not have a moment to put down her things.

Katie, without even trying, made us feel like we belonged there with her. Her welcoming nature, attending to our needs ("Would you like some coffee?"), and then showing us where we would conduct the interviews was all so generous and efficient. I loved it.

The smells coming from the kitchen made my mouth curious to know what was happening. We learned later that the morning crew, who had arrived well before the sun was up, was making everyone breakfast. It's a subtle gesture and probably one that is lost on the team at Canlis. That gesture? "We make time to share a meal together even though we have a lot to do." Anthony Bourdain, the late chef and host of the television show *Parts Unknown*, said this about meals together:

> Meals make the society, hold the fabric together in lots of way that were chasing and interesting and intoxicating to me. The perfect meal, or the best meals, occur in a context that frequently has very little to do with the food itself.

My favorite part of Bourdain's commentary is the "intoxicating" part. For me, what is intoxicating about a meal together is the enthusiasm in the multiple conversations happening at the same time. The laughter or the sadness in response to stories unfolding reveals to me the connectedness the dinner table represents. A meal together in the right context, when the guests, family, and friends are happy to sit down together, is a simple example of the peaks–end rule. The emotional peak, and there are several, comes from seeing friends enjoying each other's company, drinking wine, and laughing at absurd observations. When the context is right, a meal together is feeling valued, wanted, and welcomed all at once.

It is only fitting that our first adventure in learning about belonging at work was at a restaurant with a mission to turn people toward one another. First impressions are abundant but only once per experience. What's so inspiring to me about belonging is it can happen in any context: a retail store, a global organization, the plant floor, and even in times of disappointment. The tug of belonging is eager to show us how to live and work with one another in simple ways.

We don't need to make belonging a strategic initiative. It is always available to us in those micro-moments or grand gestures in workplace experiences. I am an idealist. But over time I have learned that in the spirit of making money, we are cruel to one another. Sometimes unintentionally and other times with disregard for others—except those in power. But despite cruelty, or because of it, belonging waits. It emerges and settles down the hurt and maximizes the joys that come from feeling valued, wanted, and welcomed.

Because of human tendencies to make messes, companies need to be intentional about shaping belonging. The whole of the workforce is likely unaware of how their life is influenced by it. When you decide to cocreate a sense of belonging, I hope your team is excited. Some will be skeptical.

But remember, belonging is something everyone craves. In a way, that makes it priceless—and a good reason to create experiences for it.

ACKNOWLEDGMENTS

T he sacrifices, thinning patience levels, delights and disappointments, and finally relief and worry, these are the range of emotions I experience when writing a book. These emotions are also experienced by those who helped bring together this book that you now hold.

Some play a supportive role, like my partner Randy, cheering me on when I really don't want to write. Encouraging me to talk through with him the ideas that are raw and need extra discussions to achieve clarity. Knowing that the house and our cat is taken care of when I sequester myself in the office is meaningful. Randy, you do this without a single complaint. You even fuel me with coffee and water and the occasional glass of wine or whiskey. I'm humbled by your kind heart.

John Willig is a storyteller. He also is my agent. John, thank you for your understanding in the many delays in writing this book. The family matters that occurred throughout writing this book were intense, sad, and, at times, overwhelming. Your support was a constant anchor in my distracted mindset.

Tim Burgard, you, like John, were supportive and understanding when I was going to be delayed, yet again. You shielded me from any frustrations that may have surfaced when I needed more time. Thank you.

Thank you, Natalie Nyquist, for making my writing more crisp. Your command of the English language is astonishing. No writer is great by himself/herself. It's a team effort to reach greatness. Am I great? Not for me to say. But you dramatically improved my writing.

When I started writing this book, I had colleagues give me guidance on the ideas and concepts you just read. Thank you, Liz Butler, Mark Babbitt, Tim Saville for your input and edits. The iconography used in this book was originally created by Nathan Grey.

To all the model companies and leaders who made time for us to come in and interview your employees and people leaders, thank you. You inspired this book. I couldn't write this book if it weren't for your generosity. It's a bit unnerving to have outsiders examine your company and culture. None of you ever flinched in what we wanted to do or the questions we asked.

Finally, thank you to my research partner, Bruce Elliot. Bruce, you brought a different perspective to the experience of belonging. Your background helped shape the concepts and gave them teeth and not just "fluffy" ideas.

As I write this section, I am watching the clock tick closer to my deadline, the time when I need to get this to HarperCollins. I know I'm forgetting to list people who helped me bring the manuscript across the finish line. Please know my omissions are a byproduct of my self-inflicted stress levels linked to finishing.

NOTES

Chapter 1: Hidden Currents

1. Michael J. Puett and Christine Gross-Loh, *The Path: What Chinese Philosophers Can Teach Us About the Good Life* (New York: Simon & Schuster, 2016), 12.

2. Alice Schroeder, *The Snowball: Warren Buffett and the Business of Life* (New York: Bantam Books, 2009), 228.

3. Warren Buffett, "To the Shareholders of Berkshire Hathaway Inc. (2010)," Berkshire Hathaway, accessed May 27, 2018, http://www.berkshirehathaway.com/letters/2010 ltr.pdf. I highly encourage all leaders to read Warren Buffett's Berkshire Hathaway annual shareholder letters. They not only contain his often-quoted wise words but also reveal the thinking and practices of one of our modern-day business giants.

4. Thomas Dreier, *We Human Chemicals: Or, the Knack of Getting Along with Everybody* (Scarsdale, NY: Updegraff Press, 1948), 25.

5. Dreier, *We Human Chemicals*, 25.

6. Warren Buffett, "My philanthropic edge," *Fortune* (blog), June 16, 2010, http://archive.fortune.com/2010/06/15 /news/newsmakers/Warren_Buffett_Pledge_Letter.fortune /index.htm.

7. Brenda Kowske, *Employee Engagement: Market Review, Buyer's Guide and Provider Profiles* (New York: Bersin & Associates, 2012).

8. Jim Carter, "Employee Engagement on the Rise in the U.S.," Gallup News, August 26, 2018, https://news.gallup.com /poll/241649/employee-engagement-rise.aspx.

9. Collins Dictionary, s.v. "monolithic (adj.)," accessed March 3, 2019, https://www.collinsdictionary.com/us/dictionary /english/monolithic.

10. Rolling Stones, *According to the Rolling Stones* (San Francisco: Chronicle Books LLC, 2003), 59.

11. Thomas Lewis, Fari Amini, and Richard Lennon, *A General Theory of Love* (New York: Vintage Books, 2000), 64.

12. Dan Siegal, "Relationship Science and Being Human," Dr. Dan Siegal, December 17, 2013, http://www.drdansiegel .com/blog/2013/12/17/relationship-science-and-being -human/.

13. Siegal, "Relationship Science and Being Human."

14. Siegal, "Relationship Science and Being Human."

15. Roy F. Baumeister and Mark R. Leary, "The Need to Belong: Desire for Interpersonal Attachments as a Fundamental Human Motivation," *Psychological Bulletin* 117, no. 3 (1995): 497–529.

16. Brené Brown, *Daring Greatly: How the Courage to Be Vulnerable Transforms the Way We Live, Love, Parent, and Lead* (New York: Gotham Books, 2012), 231–32.

17. Social Issues Research Centre, "Belonging: Research Commissioned by the Automobile Association" (SIRC, July

2007), accessed February 18, 2018, http://www.sirc.org
/publik/Belonging.pdf.

18. Carol Dweck, a psychology professor at Stanford University,
coined the term *growth mindset* and contrasted with a
fixed mindset. Her book *Mindset: Changing the Way You
Think to Fulfill Your Potential* (London: Robinson, 2017) is
essential reading for any professional or parent interested
in learning how to help people develop and grow into their
full potential.

19. Ed Frauenheim and Shawn Murphy, "A New Study Shows
That Nice Guys Finish with Higher Revenue," *Fortune*,
January 5, 2017, http://fortune.com/2017/01/05/a-new
-study-shows-that-nice-guys-finish-with-higher-revenue/#.

20. Frauenheim and Murphy, "New Study."

21. Matthew Lieberman and Naomi Eisenberger, "The Pains and
Pleasures of Social Life: A Social Cognitive Neuroscience
Approach," *Science* 323, no. 5916 (2009): 890–91.

22. James S. House, Karl R. Landis, and Debra Umberson,
"Social Relationships and Health," *Science*, New Series 241,
no. 4865 (1988): 540–45.

23. Julianne Holt-Lunstad, Timothy B. Smith, and J. Bradley
Layton, "Social Relationships and Mortality Risk: A Meta-
analytic Review," PLoS Medicine 7, no. 7 (2010), http://doi
.org/10.1371/journal.pmed.1000316.

24. Carter, "Employee Engagement."

25. Christine Porath, "Why We Need to Kick Incivility Out of
the Office," Knowledge@Wharton, June 30, 2017,
http://knowledge.wharton.upenn.edu/article/civility-at-work/.

26. Christine Porath and Christine Pearson, "The Price of
Incivility," *Harvard Business Review* (January–February
2013), https://hbr.org/2013/01/the-price-of-incivility.

27. Seunghoo Chung et al., "Friends with Performance
Benefits: A Meta-Analysis on the Relationship Between
Friendship and Group Performance," *Personality and Social
Psychology Bulletin* 44, no. 1 (2018): 63–79.

28. Rolling Stones, *According to The Rolling Stones*, 28.

Chapter 2: The Fiction in Management

1. Menéndez, Ramón, dir. *Stand and Deliver.* 1988; Burbank,
CA: Warner Bros. Pictures, 1988.

2. Richard Ryan and Edward Deci have published many
research journals on what they call self-determination
theory (SDT). A significant part of SDT is the motivating
influences of autonomy, mastery, and purpose. Edward Deci
cowrote *Why We Do What We Do: Understanding Self-Motivation*
(New York: Penguin, 1995). It's an excellent foray into
understanding SDT beyond the academic explanation of
self-motivation.

3. Rebecca Ray et al., *DNA of Engagement 2018: Moments That
Matter Throughout the Employee Life Cycle* (The Conference
Board, 2018), 4.

4. Paul Zak is a prolific research, writer, and speaker. For
more information on how empathic people and leaders
are more effective, read his book *Trust Factor: The Science of
Creating High-Performance Companies* (New York: AMACOM,
2017). See also Jorge A. Barraza et al., "Oxytocin Infusion
Increases Charitable Donations Regardless of Monetary
Resources," *Hormones and Behavior* 60, no. 2 (2011): 148–51.

5. I conducted the online survey on LinkedIn. I didn't publish
it in any groups; I simply posted the question on LinkedIn.com.
Instead of publishing the results, I used them for a keynote
I give on meaningful work.

6. Victor Frankl, *Man's Search for Meaning* (Boston: Beacon Press, 2006), 76.
7. Rob Cross, Reb Rebele, and Adam Grant, "Collaborative Overload," *Harvard Business Review* (January–February 2016), https://hbr.org/2016/01/collaborative-overload.
8. Liz Wiseman and Greg McKeown, *Multipliers: How the Best Leaders Make Everyone Smarter* (New York: HarperBusiness, 2010), 10.
9. Patrick Greenfield, "Apple Apologizes for Slowing Down Older iPhones with Aging Batteries," *The Guardian*, December 29, 2017, https://www.theguardian.com/technology/2017/dec/29/apple-apologises-for-slowing-older-iphones-battery-performance.
10. Katie Hoffman, interview by Shawn Murphy and Bruce Elliot, June 2018.
11. IBM Institute for Business Value, *Unplug from the Past*, Global C-Suite Study, 19th edition, accessed February 18, 2019, https://whirlingchief.com/wp-content/uploads/2018/06/IBM_CHRO-study-2018.pdf.

Chapter 3: The Experience of Belonging
1. Richard Thaler, "Toward a Positive Theory of Consumer Choice," *Journal of Economic Behavior and Organization* 1 (1980), 39–60, http://www.eief.it/butler/files/2009/11/thaler80.pdf.
2. Mark Canlis and Brian Canlis, interview by Shawn Murphy and Bruce Elliot, July 18, 2018.
3. Doug Conant, interview by Shawn Murphy, July 2018.
4. Diane Hamilton, "Creating Powerful Leadership Connections in the Smallest Moments with Doug Conant," Dr. Diane Hamilton, accessed February 16, 2019,

https://drdianehamilton.com/creating-powerful-leadership-connections-in-the-smallest-moments-with-doug-conant/.

5. Abram Brown, "How Campbell's Soup Went from Stale to Innovative," *Inc.*, September 14, 2011, https://www.inc.com/articles/201109/former-campbells-soup-company-ceo-doug-conant.html.

6. "Campbell Soup Company Unveils Ten-Year Plan to Reduce Childhood Obesity and Hunger in Camden," Campbell Soup Company, February 16, 2011, https://www.campbellsoupcompany.com/newsroom/press-releases/campbell-soup-company-unveils-ten-year-plan-to-reduce-childhood-obesity-and-hunger-in-camden/.

7. Doug Conant, "The Idealistic Realistic: What Really Helped Elevate Campbell Soup Company," *Harvard Business Review*, November 28, 2011, https://hbr.org/2011/11/the-flywheel-effect-what-reall.

8. David Sirota coauthored the book *The Enthusiastic Employee*. It's a worthy read for any leader interested in facilitating belonging at work.

9. Allecia Vermillion, "Brady Williams Is the New Chef at Canlis," *Seattle Met*, March 19, 2015, https://www.seattlemet.com/articles/2015/3/19/meet-brady-williams-the-new-chef-at-canlis-march-2015.

10. Cristina Filippo, "Are You Hiring for Cultural Fit or Cultural Contribution?," Impact Potential, February 4, 2016, http://www.impactpotential.com/blog/m.blog/36/are-you-hiring-for-cultural-fit-or-cultural-contribution.

11. Hoffman, interview.

12. Amanda Lynn Sullivan, interview by Shawn Murphy, Canlis Restaurant, Seattle, WA, July 18, 2018.

Chapter 4: The Outsiders

1. Sierra College, Okei Ito, *Journal of Sierra Nevada History &* *Biography*, 5, no. 1 (Winter 2013): https://www.sierra college.edu/ejournals/jsnhb/v5n1/ito.html.

2. Brené Brown, *Braving the Wilderness: The Quest for True Belonging and the Courage to Stand Alone* (New York: Random House, 2017), 16.

3. Carolyn Parkinson, Adam M. Kleinbaum, and Thalia Wheatley, "Similar Neural Responses Predict Friendship," *Nature Communications* 9, article 332 (2018).

4. Matthew D. Lieberman, "Birds of a Feather Synchronize Together," *Trends in Cognitive Sciences* 22, no. 5 (2018), 371–72.

5. *Dead Poets Society*, Peter Weir (director), Touchstone Pictures, Silver Screen Partners IV (Burbank), 1989.

6. Noah Kirsch, "The Inside Story of Papa John's Toxic Culture," *Forbes*, July 19, 2018, https://www.forbes.com /sites/forbesdigitalcovers/2018/07/19/the-inside-story-of -papa-johns-toxic-culture/.

7. Julie Creswell, Kevin Draper, Rachel Abrams, "At Nike, Revolt Led by Women Leads to Exodus of Male Executives," *New York Times*, April 28, 2018, https://www.nytimes.com /2018/04/28/business/nike-women.html.

8. Creswell, Draper, and Abrams, "Revolt Led by Women."

9. Michael Housman and Dylan Minor, "Toxic Workers," (working paper, Harvard Business School, 2015).

10. Housman and Minor, "Toxic Workers."

11. Ståle Einarsen and Helge Hoel, "The Negative Acts Questionnaire: Development, Validation and Revision of Bullying at Work," 2001.

12. Samuel Farly, "The Measurement and Impact of Workplace Cyberbullying" (PhD diss., University of Sheffield, 2015), http://etheses.whiterose.ac.uk/11652/.

13. Wilmar B. Schaufeli and Arnold B. Bakker, "Job Demands, Job Resources, and Their Relationship with Burnout and Engagement: A Multisample Study," *Journal of Organizational Behavior* 25 (2004): 293–315, https://www.evernote.com/l /AAWtShqwBEhH4Zgp1-ZDpR161IjmqMsY2zk.

14. Sabrina Ruggieri et al., "Cyberball: The Impact of Ostracism on the Well-Being of Early Adolescents," *Swiss Journal of Psychology* 72, no. 2 (2013): 103–9.

15. D. Lance Feris, Huiwen Lian, Douglas J. Brown, and Rachel Morrison, "Ostracism, Self-Esteem, and Job Performance: When Do We Self-Verify and When Do We Self-Enhance?" *Academy of Management Journal*, 58, no. 1 (2015): 279–97.

16. Kristen Weir, "The Pain of Social Rejection," *American Psychological Association* 43, no. 4 (April 2012): 50, http://www.apa.org/monitor/2012/04/rejection.aspx.

17. Timothy Deckman and Richard S. Pond Jr., "Belongingness as a Core Personality Trait: How Social Exclusion Influences Social Functioning and Personality Expression," *Journal of Personality* 79, no. 6 (December 2011): 1281–314.

18. Deckman and Pond, "Belongingness as a Core Personality Trait," 1281–314.

19. Art Kleiner, "The Thought Leader Interview: Doug Conant," Strategy+Business (blog), August 28, 2012, https://www.strategy-business.com/article/00128?gko=50b48.

Chapter 5: Of the Ways of Misfits, Mavericks, and Renegades

1. Aristotle, *Nicomachean Ethics* (Indianapolis/Cambridge: Hacket Publishing Company, Inc., 1999.) Kindle.
2. Marilyn B. Brewer, "The Social Self: On Being the Same and Different at the Same Time," *Personality and Social Psychology Bulletin* 17, no. 5 (1991): 475–82. https://doi.org/10.1177%2F0146167291175001.
3. Tip Kindall, interview by Shawn Murphy, July 9, 2018.
4. *The Container Store 2017 Annual Report*, PDF, 5, accessed September 6, 2018, http://investor.containerstore.com/financial-reports/annual/default.aspx.
5. Kindall, interview.
6. Kindall, interview.
7. Robert Steven Kaplan, *What to Ask the Person in the Mirror: Critical Questions for Becoming a More Effective Leader and Reaching Your Potential* (Boston: Harvard Business Review Press, 2011).
8. Sullivan, interview.
9. Brené Brown, "Finding our way to true belonging," Ideas. Ted.com (blog), September 11, 2017, https://ideas.ted.com/finding-our-way-to-true-belonging/.
10. Psychologists have a different set of terms than what I use. Adaptors are high self-monitors and Maintainers are low self-monitors. There's a large body of research that has tested the validity of the two personality types. For more detailed explanations of the two types, I recommend starting with reading Richard Lennox and Raymond Wolfe, David Day and Deidra Schleicher.
11. David V. Day and Deidra J. Schleicher, "Self-Monitoring at Work: A Motive-Based Perspective," *Journal of Personality* 74, no. 3 (June 2006): 685–713.

12. Stephen J. Zacarro, Roseanne J. Foti, and David A, Kenny, "Self-Monitoring and Trait-Based Variance in Leadership: An Investigation in Leader Flexibility Across Multiple Group Situations," in *Key Readings in Social Psychology, Small Groups*, edited by John M. Levine and Richard L. Moreland (New York: Psychology Press, 2016), 357–367.

13. While the terms adapters and maintainers are my labels, the terms are linked to a large body of research. David V. Day and Deidra J. Schleicher, "Self-Monitoring at Work: A Motive Based Perspective," *Journal of Personality*, 74, no. 3 (June 2006): 685–713.

14. Brandon Rigoni and Jim Asplund, "Strengths-Based Employee Development: The Business Result," Gallup (blog), July 7, 2016, https://www.gallup.com /workplace/236297/strengths-based-employee -development-business-results.aspx.

15. Based on numbers pulled from the Bureau of Labor and Statistics website (https://www.bls.gov/) using August 2018 full-time employment numbers.

16. Gallup, *2015 State of the American Manager*, 8.

17. Gallup, *2017 State of the American Manager*, 6.

18. Kevin Rose et al., "Skunked: An Integrative Review Exploring the Consequences of the Dysfunctional Leader and Implications for Those Employees Who Work for Them," *Human Resource Development Review* 14, no. 1 (March 2015), 64–90.

19. For the full list of dysfunctional behaviors see Rose et al., "Skunked."

20. Peter F. Drucker, *Managing Oneself* (Boston: Harvard Business Review Press, 2017).

21. Drucker, *Managing Oneself.*

Chapter 6: Fallacies, Foes, and Tech-Fueled Friendships

1. Glenn Rifkin, "Where We'll Work," *Korn Ferry Briefings*, no. 25: 40–49.
2. Adam J. Guastella, Philip B. Mitchell, and Mark R. Dadds, "Oxytocin Increases Gaze to the Eye Region of Human Faces," *Biological Psychiatry* 63, no. 1 (January 2008): 3–5; Michael Kosfeld et al., "Oxytocin Increases Trust in Humans," *Nature* 435 (June 2005): 673–76; Paul J. Zak, Angela A. Stanton, and Sheila Ahmadi, "Oxytocin Increases Generosity in Humans," PLoS ONE 2, no. 11 (2007).
3. Adam Piore, "What Technology Can't Change About Happiness: As Pills and Gadgets Proliferate, What Matters Is Still Social Connection," *Nautilus*, no. 28 (September 2015), http://nautil.us/issue/28/2050/what-technology-cant-change-about-happiness.
4. Peter Jackson, interview by Shawn Murphy, August 23, 2018.
5. Jackson, interview.
6. Piore, "What Technology Can't Change About Happiness."
7. Alvaro Pascual-Leone, "The Plastic Human Brain Cortex," *Annual Review of Neuroscience* 28 (2005): 377–401.
8. Pascual-Leone, "The Plastic Human Brain Cortex."
9. Scott Ard, "Mark Zuckerberg's IPO Letter: Why Facebook Exists," Yahoo! Finance, February 1, 2012, https://finance.yahoo.com/news/mark-zuckerberg%E2%80%99s-ipo-letter--why-facebook-exists.html.
10. *The Future of Jobs: Employment, Skills, and Workforce Strategy for the Fourth Industrial Revolution* (World Economic Forum, 2016), http://www3.weforum.org/docs/WEF_Future_of_Jobs.pdf.
11. Adam Gazzaley, "The Cognition Crisis," Medium, July 9, 2018, https://medium.com/s/futurehuman/the-cognition-crisis-a1482e889fcb.

12. Emma Seppälä and Marissa King, "Burnout at Work Isn't Just About Exhaustion. It's Also About Loneliness," *Harvard Business Review*, June 29, 2017, https://hbr.org/2017/06/burnout-at-work-isnt-just-about-exhaustion-its-also-about-loneliness.

13. Dan Gouthro, "The Employee Burnout Crisis: Study Reveals Big Workplace Challenge in 2017," Kronos, January 9, 2017, https://www.kronos.com/about-us/newsroom/employee-burnout-crisis-study-reveals-big-workplace-challenge-2017.

14. Mollie Lombardi, "Moving Beyond Burnout: Strategies to Sustain Engagement and Retain Workers," Kronos, accessed February 18, 2019, https://www.kronos.com/resources/moving-beyond-burnout-strategies-sustain-engagement-and-retain-workers.

15. Lombardi, "Moving Beyond Burnout."

16. Lombardi, "Moving Beyond Burnout."

17. Jacques Bughin, et al., "Skill Shift: Automation and the Future of the Workforce," McKinsey Global Institute, May 2018, https://www.mckinsey.com/featured-insights/future-of-work/skill-shift-automation-and-the-future-of-the-workforce.

18. Lynda Gratton, "The Challenge of Scaling Soft Skills," Sloan Review MIT (blog), August 6, 2018, https://sloanreview.mit.edu/article/the-challenge-of-scaling-soft-skills/.

Chapter 7: Feeling Valued

1. Hunter Powell, interview by Shawn Murphy on September 8, 2018.

2. "Jim Self," USC Thornton School of Music, accessed February 16, 2019, http://music.usc.edu/jim-self.

3. Jim Self, interview by Shawn Murphy, December 5, 2018.

4. Self, interview.

5. Sullivan, interview.

6. Kip Tindell, interview by Shawn Murphy, The Container Store, July 12, 2018.

7. Eric L. Garland et al., "Upward Spirals of Positive Emotions Counter Downward Spirals of Negativity: Insights from the Broaden-and-Build Theory and Affective Neuroscience on the Treatment of Emotion Dysfunctions and Deficits in Psychopathology," *Clinical Psychology Review* 30, no. 7 (November 2010): 849–64.

8. Christopher R. Madan, "Positive Emotion Enhances Association-Memory," *Emotion* (April 2018), 2.

9. Garland, "Upward Spirals of Positive Emotions."

10. The three-quarters of the workforce reference is linked to Gallup's engagement studies. Jim Harter, "Employee Engagement on the Rise," Gallup, August 26, 2018, https://news.gallup.com/poll/241649/employee -engagement-rise.aspx.

11. Employee interviews by Shawn Murphy and Bruce Elliot, LinkedIn office, San Francisco, CA, June 19, 2018.

Chapter 8: Feeling Wanted

1. *Star Wars: Episode VI–Return of the Jedi* (1983).

2. John Stuart Mill famously contrasted the better parts of humanity against our faults. The fool and the pig represent our faults. Mill used Socrates as an example of humanity's upstanding citizen who acted in the best interest of the greater good. Mill's book *Utilitarianism* (1863) delves into the philosophical underpinnings of utility and its application to politics and social matters. Over time many researchers and thought leaders have expanded our understanding of utility,

for example Daniel Kahneman. I have combined Mill's
assertions with the contemporary work of Kahneman.

3. Carey K. Morewedge, "Utility: Anticipated, Experienced,
and Remembered," in *The Wiley Blackwell Handbook of
Judgement and Decision Making*, edited by Gideon Keen and
George Wu, 1st ed. (Mariden, MA: John Wiley & Sons,
2015), 295–330.

4. Barbara L. Fredrickson, "Extracting Meaning from Past
Affective Experiences: The Importance of Peaks, Ends, and
Specific Emotions," *Cognition and Emotion* 14, no. 4 (2000):
577–606.

5. Fredrickson, "Extracting Meaning," 577–606.

6. Items one through five from Fredrickson, "Extracting
Meaning," 577–606.

7. Item number six from Morewedge, "Utility: Anticipated,
Experienced, and Remembered," 295–330.

8. Kory Floyd, "What Lack of Affection Can Do to You,"
Psychology Today, August 31, 2013, https://www.psychology
today.com/us/blog/affectionado/201308/what-lack
-affection-can-do-you.

9. Way H. Greem, Magda Campbell, and Raphael David,
"Psychosocial Dwarfism: A Critical Review of the Evidence,"
Journal of the American Academy of Child Psychiatry 23, no. 1
(1984): 39–48.

10. Sullivan, interview.

11. Brent Stewart, interview by Shawn Murphy, Barry-
Wehmiller, July 24, 2018.

12. Rosanna Duruthy, interview by Shawn Murphy, LinkedIn,
San Francisco, CA, August, 17, 2018.

13. It's unclear who coined the phrase "time to wow." I learned
about it through a product development team I'm part of

at Bluescape. It's been attributed to David Skok, and he attributes it to the former CEO of Constant Contact, Gail Goodman. You can read more of Skok's take on "time to wow" here: https://www.forentrepreneurs.com/time-to -wow/. It is important to note that I am not referring to the idea in the way Skok and others have.

14. B. Joseph Pine and James H. Gilmore's book *The Experience Economy* (Boston, MA: Harvard Business Review Press, 2011) lays out their framework in an easy-to-understand manner.

15. B. Joseph Pine and James H. Gilmore, "Satisfaction, Sacrifice, and Surprise: Three Small Steps Create One Giant Leap into the Experience Economy," *Strategy & Leadership* 28, no. 1 (2000), 18–23.

16. Pine and Gilmore, "Satisfaction, Sacrifice, and Surprise."

17. Pine and Gilmore, "Satisfaction, Sacrifice, and Surprise."

Chapter 9: Feeling Welcomed

1. Chad Balthrop is a pastor at First Baptist Owasso in Oklahoma. On January 4, 2019, I asked my family and friends via Facebook the question that opens this chapter.

2. Paul Zak, interview by Shawn Murphy, August 10, 2018. Oxytocin is a neuropeptide that the brain releases to signal bonding and trustworthy behaviors. Paul Zak's work is prolific and useful to any leader who wants to remain relevant in business. You can read Paul's books, *Trust Factor* (AMACOM, 2017) and the *Moral Molecule* (Dutton, 2013) to understand how oxytocin influences the way we work together, love one another, and, ultimately, achieve great success when we understand the human need to belong. You can also view his TED talk "Trust, Morality—and Oxytocin?" (https://www.ted.com/talks/paul_zak_trust

_morality_and_oxytocin?) to understand the importance and relevance of his research.

3. Zak, interview.
4. Mark Canlis and Brian Canlis, interview by Bruce Elliot and Shawn Murphy, Canlis Restaurant, Seattle, WA, June 14, 2018.
5. Annamarie Mann, "Why We Need Best Friends at Work," Gallup, January 15, 2018, https://www.gallup.com /workplace/236213/why-need-best-friends-work.aspx.
6. Chung et al., "Friends with Performance Benefits," 63–79.
7. Chung et al., "Friends with Performance Benefits," 63–79.
8. Lewis Garrad, interview by Shawn Murphy, July 12, 2018.
9. Adam M. Grant and Francesca Gino, "A Little Thanks Goes a Long Way: Explaining Gratitude Expressions Motivate Prosocial Behavior," *Journal of Personality and Social Psychology* 98, no. 6 (2010), 946–55.
10. Grant and Gino, "A Little Thanks Goes a Long Way."

Chapter 10: When Companies Care

1. Rob Brunner, "I'm a Shepherd and I'm a Warrior," *Fast Company* (April 2017), 58.
2. "Nielsen, Chobani Leads in US Yogurt Market Share," SmartBrief, March 13, 2017, https://www.smartbrief.com/ s/2017/03/nielsen-chobani-leads-us-yogurt-market-share.
3. "Greek Yogurt Market Share of Chobani in the United States from 2012 to 2017," Statista, December 2017, https://www .statista.com/statistics/268342/greek-yogurt-market-share-of -chobani-in-the-us/.
4. "Chobani LLC: Company Overview," Great Place to Work, https://www.greatplacetowork.com/certified-company /5003408.

5. Aaron Hurst et al., *2016 Global Report: Purpose at Work* (Imperative and LinkedIn, 2016), https://business.linkedin .com/content/dam/me/business/en-us/talent-solutions/ resources/pdfs/purpose-at-work-global-report.pdf.

6. Tindell, interview.

7. Eben Harrell, "How 1% Performance Improvements Led to Olympic Gold," *Harvard Business Review*, October 30, 2015, https://hbr.org/2015/10/how-1-performance -improvements-led-to-olympic-gold.

8. *Candid advantage* is a term that is also used by Jonah Berger and Alixandra Barash. Their usage applies to candid selfies. Our use of *candid advantage* is solely applied to candor and feedback.

Chapter 11: Captains of Context

1. Rhonda Spencer, interview by Shawn Murphy, Barry-Wehmiller.

2. Canlis and Barry-Wehmiller employee interviews by Shawn Murphy.

INDEX

ABOUT THE AUTHOR

SHAWN MURPHY has been listed as a top leadership speaker by Inc.com. He was handpicked by IBM to be part of a futurist group on new ways of working. He has nearly 30 years of consulting experience in advising executives on designing large-scale change projects. His first book, *The Optimistic Workplace*, was nominated as business book of the year. Currently, Shawn is the Director of Organizational Development and Workplace Trends at Silicon Valley tech-company Bluescape. He lives in San Francisco.